Ian Jenkins was born and bred in Sheffield making him fluent in English and broad Yorkshire as well as not using 100 words when 10 will do. His recent retirement at the age of 55 allowed him more time to enjoy his love of sports, especially football, golf, cricket, cycling and open water swimming and to put into writing, in his unique self-deprecating humorous style, his experience of cycling from Lands End to John O'Groats.

To all those who contributed to this book and inspired me to write it.

Ian Jenkins

HOW HARD CAN IT BE?

AUSTIN MACAULEY PUBLISHERS™

LONDON • CAMBRIDGE • NEW YORK • SHARJAH

A CIP catalogue record for this title is available from the British Library.

ISBN 9781398471382 (Paperback)
ISBN 9781398471399 (ePub e-book)

www.austinmacauley.com

First Published 2023
Austin Macauley Publishers Ltd®
1 Canada Square
Canary Wharf
London
E14 5AA

Table of Contents

Chapter 1
Day 1 – Here We Go

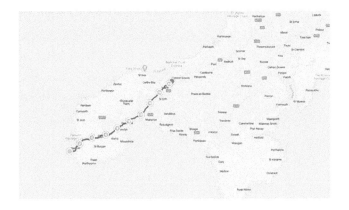

Six o'clock and the alarm goes off. Nothing unusual in that. Nothing usual either. For the last 20 years, the alarm has been going off at any time between 4 am and 8 am depending on whether my work was taking me to London, Milton Keynes, Manchester or any other town or city in the UK that required the latest communications technology. Strangely enough, Manchester, at only 43 miles, was the one that needed the earliest start. What always started as one of the most beautiful and scenic drives to work anyone could wish for, over the Snake Pass in Derbyshire always descended in to a 90-minute crawl through the outskirts of the city for the last 10 miles.

Today was different though. Today I was booked on the 9.06 train to Penzance. Not just me, me and my bike because once I got to Penzance and a short 10-mile taxi ride to Lands End, we were going to embark on a little adventure to John O'Groats, a mere 900 miles away (depending on who you ask!) using nothing but our own steam and technology.

I had got everything prepared the night before so just needed to add a few last things to the saddle bags and I'd be ready. This was no organised, supported trip. As I said, just me and the bike so I needed to be frugal on what I was taking with me. This wasn't too much of a problem as by my reckoning, I would need bike gear to ride in during the day and sleep at night. Just minimal casual wear for an evening meal and a pint each night.

I had breakfast with my 12-year-old son, Ben, and dropped him off at school, just under two miles up the hill, at 8 o'clock. He would often walk but I figured that as I would not see him for the best part of two weeks, then those last few minutes with him would be precious. Sharon, my wife, left for work at the same time. When I got back home from the school run, the house was empty and silent so I had a moment to reflect on what I was about to do.

Well, it's too late to back out now, so I locked up, got the bike out of the garage and cycled around to Chesterfield train station, which is at least two minutes away, and boarded the 9.06 to Penzance (changing at Plymouth).

The bike was pre-booked to be stored on the train (there is probably another book in describing how that gets done) and so I got on coach D to store it. For anyone who remembers the '80s' game show, *The Krypton Factor*, trying to get the bike in the compartment was just like one of their challenges. The host, Gordon Burns, would have not been impressed, but 10 minutes later it was installed and I went to clean the oil off my hands!

Seat 50 in coach C was blindly reserved for me. When I got there, it was facing backwards, not next to the window, no table and someone sat next to me. The rest of the carriage was rammed full. There was only one option – an upgrade to a seat in coach A (1st class)!

The rest of the journey went as planned and I got to Plymouth with 10 minutes spare to get on to the Penzance train which was done with no major drama. Plymouth to Penzance is a two-hour journey and not only was there not a special compartment for the bike, or any spare seats next to an empty one, there was no first class either. I'm having a crisis already and I've not even started!

I make the best of it and park the bike on one side of the carriage and my ample backside on the other next to an older bloke and so as not to appear sociable, I got the earphones in and the iPod banging out some music fairly smartish, only to be tapped on the shoulder by some Lycra-clad cyclist. You can always tell the keen ones as they have a proper club top on, in this case royal blue with a thick yellow band across the middle – think Boca Juniors of the cycling fraternity – which, going by the logo emblazoned across it, is the kit of choice of Chester CC.

"You doing the end to end?" (First chapter and I'm already using the chuffing lingo!)

"Yes."

Now, a simple single word answer of "yes" to most people would normally mean, "Yes, but I'm busy listening to Jackson Browne and I'm a miserable sod, so don't say anything else."

Somehow, that got lost in translation and he heard:

"Yes, let's talk more about it!"

And out came his maps, hundreds of the buggers, he even told me what scale they were all in and everything. He asked me what maps I had, so I just held up my iPhone (well it was 2011, why would I need a paper map) and anyway how hard can it be, to start with you just keep going east with a bit of north every now and again and then at Bristol swap around and keep going north with a bit of east.

But this guy was a proper cycling nerd. He'd only gone and studied ordinance survey maps and plotted his route to go along valleys rather than up and down hills! Pah, what a lightweight. Me, I've gone on the AA auto route, banged in Lands End to John O'Groats by the shortest route avoiding motorways and that's the way I'm going. If there's hills, there's hills. For every uphill, there's a downhill. Simple!

Two hours later, I arrived in Penzance and got a taxi to Lands End. (The Chester CC man was cycling there!) A quick photo shoot with the Cuban in the hut by the mileage post thingy (local jobs for local people!) and off I went on the first leg of the 900-mile trip.

I got to Penzance without any problems, a few minor hills but nothing major and then decided to listen to the Chester nerd who had recommended NCN3 – National Cycling Network – flatter and a great path along the coast (I would literally have fallen in to the sea if I had come off) but a couple of miles further. Then on to Hayle with one very minor wrong turn and started off towards the hotel. But decided I was going the wrong way so I turned around and went the other way. Then found out I was going the right way after all! About three miles extra and if I carry on like this, then 900 miles could very quickly become 1000! Oh, for the days of paper maps.

But, 24 miles is in the bag, I am in the hotel and tomorrow has 68 miles in store so an early night is in order.

Ready to go at Lands End

After posting the day's events on my blog, there was then a short exchange of messages between various readers.

JK – *Hi Ian, enjoying the blog. It's hilarious but how do we know you're not holed up with room service in a Holiday Inn Express somewhere? To persuade a Yorkshireman to part with his hard-earned cash I would like to see a photo of you sweating and blowing, clad in lycra and in the middle of some windswept god-forsaken nowhere in the rain.*

Keep rollin', rollin', rollin' – RAWHIDE.

My Reply – *James, you may very well be right, there really is no way of proving anything other than following me. There is a sort of approved thing where you get a card and get it stamped at loads of post offices on the way, but I'm not farting about like that and anyway, I could always have just driven in between. I think back to that sales conference when Matthew Pinsent came and handed his medals around. When asked if he was frightened, they might get nicked, he said, "No, because I'll know I was still Olympic champion." I sort of see it like that, I could cheat but at the end of it all, only I will know if I did it or not.*

So, get your hand in your pocket or I'll let everyone know that you've been requesting photos of me clad in Lycra!!!

JK – *OK, good point. He looked like an Olympic Champion though…*

Good Luck on the hills and try those ice baths like Eddie Izzard. I'll sponsor you 5 minutes in one of them

A&P W – *Only 820 miles to go. Sleep well P and A x*

JS – *Well done Mr J! Hope tomorrow goes well too!*

P.S I am getting even less schoolwork done now I have your blog page to comment on as well as facebook to update...oh technological advancements!

SJ – *it wasn't the lycra bit that worried me, it's the fact he wanted a photo of you sweating and blowing!*

AB – *So funny SJ, to be fair I'm hooked! The whole blog is hilarious x.*

Chapter 2
Planning and Dilemmas

So, that's the first day done, got myself to Lands End and started cycling just as per the plan.

But what was the plan?

The first thing was the route and places to stay overnight. As I said earlier, AA auto route was my route planner of choice and as I reckoned, it was around 844 miles to be done over 11 days (ten full and two half) then I just divided it in to 844 and calculated I should be looking to stay overnight every 80 miles or so.

This coupled with my early thoughts on speed which were 10mph, then I would break the day up in to four segments

First ride = 8 am to 10 am

30-minute break

Second ride = 10.30 am to 12.30 pm

1-hour lunch break

Third ride = 1.30 pm to 3.30 pm

30-minute break

Fourth ride = 4 pm to 6 pm

That would leave me with four hours at the end of the day to get showered and changed, get some tea and have a relatively early night. And so I pre-booked a hotel roughly every 80 miles. Not as easy as I first thought because I didn't want to be cycling any further than necessary "off route" to get to the hotel and once I got past Glasgow, it was a case of "stay where there is civilisation".

Which is why I ended up booking the following schedule (based mainly on where Premier Inns were!)

Day 1 – Mon 6 June – Lands End to Hayle (19 miles)

Day 2 – Tue 7 June – Hayle to Sourton Cross (76 miles)

Day 3 – Wed 8 June – Sourton Cross to Bristol Airport (80 miles)

Day 4 – Thurs 9 June – Bristol Airport to Worcester (75 miles)

Day 5 – Fri 10 June – Worcester to Knutsford (88 miles)

Day 6 – Sat 11 June – Knutsford to Kendal (80 miles)

Day 7 – Sun 12 June – Kendal to Dumcrieff (84 miles)

Day 8 – Mon 13 June – Dumcrieff to Loch Lomond (71 miles)

Day 9 – Tue 14 June – Loch Lomond to Fort William (87 miles)

Day 10 – Wed 15 June – Fort William to Inverness (66 miles)

Day 11 – Thurs 16 June – Inverness to Dunbeath (80 miles)

Day 12 – Fri 17 June – Dunbeath to John O'Groats (38 miles)

Charity

The first thing people ask when you tell them you are doing this (after why!) is, "What cause are you doing it for?" Raising money really wasn't the intention and it would just be another thing to organise. At the time I was managing a local under-13s football team and it did occur to me that we could do with a few extra pennies in the coffers but after one local charity showed me how much they needed support, I decided that predominantly healthy kids who might have to wear slightly different shorts to some of their teammates would be fine as they were and I would try and raise some money to help kids for whom playing football, of any sort, in any kit, was just a dream.

The two charities I decided to raise money for were "Amy's House" which is a small local charity in Sheffield that provides respite care for Children with special needs and the National Rheumatoid Arthritis Society which supports sufferers of this crippling disease as well as helping look for a cure for a disability which could not only affect every single one of us but is also the largest single cause of disabilities in Children under 16.

I was also adamant that all and every penny of any money raised would go to these charities and all expenses for the trip including bike, hotels, food and Mars Bars would be funded by myself. In addition, whilst using the *Just Giving* fundraising web site, I also wanted to create an old-fashioned kind of sponsorship where you were rewarded for the results rather than for trying. And therefore, I made the commitment that of the 844 miles I was due to travel, any of the trip that I didn't complete, I would pay out of my own pocket. So if you sponsored me for say £20 and I only got halfway, then I would refund half of your sponsorship money whilst the charity didn't suffer.

I also committed to updating a blog at the end of each day's cycling, updating everyone on progress, anything interesting that had happened during the day and any thoughts that passed through my mind whilst sat in the saddle for eight hours a day.

Equipment

I'd better start by looking at a bike. I had an old mountain bike in the garage that I was pretty sure wouldn't do the job and so I took myself to a couple of local large bike shops. As soon as my 18 stone walked through the door and they realised I wasn't buying for a child, then they weren't interested. I tried to teach myself what more money got for you but other than the weight of the frame I couldn't work it out. What on earth do you get for £10,000 that you don't for £200 on a piece of equipment that, to the untrained eye, looks exactly the same?

I was starting to get a bit disheartened and going off the whole idea when I came across what can best be described as a wooden hut selling bikes in a town called Matlock which is around 10 miles from where I live. Stanley Fearn Cycles.

I walked in and was met by a very friendly chap asking how he could help me.

"Don't laugh," I started, "but I'm doing Lands End to John O'Groats and haven't got a clue where to start with a bike."

"Why would I laugh?"

"Well for starters I don't exactly look like a cyclist, never mind one who is going to do LEJOG and I've not done much or got time to do much training."

"I shouldn't worry about that, mate," was his answer to that. "Are you a complete couch potato or do you do a bit of exercise?"

I gave him chapter and verse of how I play golf and train a kid's football team which was all he needed to hear.

"You'll be fine. As long as you spend enough time on the bike to make yourself comfortable with it, controlling it, changing gears etc. then you'll train as you go. First couple of days you'll get by on adrenaline. The third or fourth day will be harder when that runs dry but by the fifth day you'll have done near on 300 miles of training on the trip. Go for it."

He then took me through various options and what costs money and what doesn't. The weight of the frame, the gears, the brakes, etc. all can vary massively in cost. I was prepared to pay a bit for a lightweight frame because I'd got enough weight to carry as it was. Similar with the gears. I'd always had a bike from being a kid and the chain getting jammed in the gears was always a pain so if we could stop that from happening, then let's pay a bit extra to do it. Brakes, however, were a different matter. Not once in the history of me riding a bike had I pulled on the brakes and the bike had failed to stop, so there was no way I was paying extra for fancy brakes.

The next discussion was mountain bike or road bike. He asked about the route and explained the pros and cons of each. Road bike would be better on roads but may cause problems with punctures and wheel problems if I strayed off tarmac. Mountain bikes are good on any terrain but would be harder work on tarmac given the amount of tyre rubber connected to the road. In the end he recommended a Trek Hybrid bike. As the name would lead you to expect, it's more robust than a road bike with slightly thicker tyres but nowhere near the weight and tyres of a mountain bike.

Final question, one which had never even entered my head, "Drop handlebars or flat?"

No idea. He asked what the main driver was for me doing the trip and when I explained about the newspaper article and seeing a bit of the country, he said that it was a no-brainer.

"You don't want to be hunched over the front of the bike looking at the floor then. Flat handlebars it is."

£750 all in. Probably four times more than I'd ever paid for a bike before but nothing compared to some of the eye watering prices you see for the top of the range stuff.

Training regime

This will be short. As I had planned to do this in four stints of 20 miles a day then that would be my training plan. There was a decent route from home that went in a loop of around 15 miles. Near enough to 20. And given that I was working and doing the kid's football and trying to fit some golf in, then four times a week rather than four times a day would do the trick.

For the last two weeks, I put the bags on the bike and stuck a brick on either side to simulate what I'd be carrying. That was fun until I got used to it. Any slight leaning to one side or the other and the Bricks had a tendency to want to take over and make that lean in to a full-blown fall!

What else did I need?

On the assumption that my daily attire for riding would be, from the bottom up: a pair of socks, a pair of pants, cycling shorts and a T-shirt (brightly coloured for safety), I figured I'd need two sets of shorts and T-shirts for riding in. I could sort of wash the one I'd been wearing at the end of each day and just in case it hadn't quite dried, then I could wear the other one for the day after. I'd also invested in a pair of cycling tights and an under armour just in case we had any cold days. Finally, I had a very lightweight, fluorescent waterproof top, just in case. I say waterproof; showerproof would probably be stretching it a bit!

The clip-on cycling shoes would suffice for the ride but I'd need something to wear at night so I found a pair of very lightweight Puma trainers that were perfect. It was just like having a bit of cloth wrapped around your feet which given they would be in the bag during the day, the lighter the better. A pair of shorts for the evenings along with trackie bottoms again in case its cold and a couple of T-shirts to wear on alternative nights and away we go.

Oh, and underwear.

I was a genius. Here was the plan. Before I set off, I will send a pair of clean pants and socks to each of the hotels I am staying in along with a pre-paid envelope back home. When I get to the hotel, I can pick up the envelope, put on the clean underwear and put the dirty pair in the pre-paid envelope back home. No need to carry them the length of the UK with me!

However, I'd sorted my first mid-life crisis out by now and was living back home with my wife and son.

"If you think I'm waking up every morning to a pair of your dirty pants on the floor at the bottom of the stairs, then you'd better think again." (This was in the days when the post came in the morning not at 4.30 in the afternoon which it seems to be these days.)

So, 12 pairs of socks and underwear went in the bag as well. I ditched the ones I'd worn at the hotel every night so at least as I went along, the weight in the bag was dropping!

There were also a few other, seemingly minor decisions that were keeping me up at night. 844 miles is 844 miles, nothing I can do about that but what should I do about these?

The bell dilemma

As those who had seen me just prior to the ride would have noticed, losing weight off my stomach to make the ride easier wasn't exactly a success, so I was looking at additional ways of reducing the weight. Reflectors had been removed (it's practically light 24 hours in June!) and the bell is sitting there looking at me.

Not that it weighs a great deal but every little helps. But the real dilemma is – what is the point?

Health and Safety would have you believe that it's an essential safety device and gives you the chance to warn those about to walk out in to the road having not heard or seen you, but I don't agree.

For a start, I can always shout "oi", something in which I am well-practiced, but the bell says two things to me, both very contradictory and neither much use.

Firstly, it's a thing for old women, a device you'd expect Miss Marple to have on her bike and I'm loath to come across like that.

But secondly, there is no polite way of ringing a bell. It just has a sort of aggressive ring to it. Some lycra lout on a mountain bike rang their bell at me the other day when they wanted to pass me on the canal path while I was dawdling along looking at the newly hatched chicks and all of a sudden, I went from a peaceful chap enjoying nature to bike rage all in the ring of a bell. If he'd shouted "get out of the ****** way" at me, I'm sure I'd have been less angry.

So, on reflection, I think the bell is going to get removed unless anyone can give a sensible case to retain it.

PB – It is a legal requirement mate! Wouldn't want you using getting locked up as an excuse!

PW – Al says she's got a kid's bike siren in the garage if you want to borrow it. Gets over the Miss Marple issue –

plays emergency services sounds, so guess it would get people to move pretty quickly! Doesn't weigh much either!

To lube or not to lube

Very sensitive subject this one. Common opinion seems to be that 8–10 hours a day in the saddle for 12 days is going to take its toll on my backside and that I need to take action to protect it.

Well there is some cream designed for just such an issue…Chamois Butt'r it's called and I've got a tube in the bag ready.

But (no pun intended) I just can't bring myself to lube up my backside…it's just not right is it…what if I get hijacked, deliverance style, by some hairy bikers in the middle of Exmoor…I've practically done half the job for them and it would make resistance very difficult! Some have advised that if I am hijacked, then it's inevitable what will happen and it will just make it easier on me. I'm not convinced and for now I'm thinking the ample padding I already have on my backside should suffice and the cream can stay in the bag!

B – Without a doubt lube up but keep an eye out (no pun intended) for Hairy Bikers. If they do manage to catch up with you, and you are not too shaken after they have done the deed, can you get me a copy of their Chicken & Mushroom pie recipe?

PB – Chaffing would be a nightmare with all that time in the saddle, suggest adding Vaseline as well. Could be the least of your worries though as a pal of mine who does a LOT of cycling alerted me to the condition known as "Genital Numbness" and you don't want that!

It has to be said though that in attempting such a feat some would say that you may be suffering from Cranial numbness.

Good luck mate.

The Helmet

When I was a kid, bike helmets weren't even invented…in fact I don't think even motorcyclists had to wear them and as a casual cyclist as an adult, I never wore one.

However, 844 miles and every single ounce of common sense in me says I should wear a helmet. But interestingly enough, research has shown that cyclists without a helmet are statistically safer than those with! Apparently because those not wearing one have an increased sense of safety and take more precautions but also because those driving cars, vans, lorries etc see those without a helmet as more vulnerable and so give them more room.

All things considered though, I've decided to wear one and here's why…

I have invested in some fancy dan shoes which clip into inch-wide pedals designed for the shoes. This is supposed to make you go faster because not only are you putting energy in to pushing the pedal down with each foot, you are also doing so pulling it back up (although in my experience it knocks about 0.5 seconds off a 10-mile ride!)

But….and it's a big but…occasionally you (i.e. me) forget to unclip your feet prior to stopping and all off a sudden you are tipping one way or the other, Frank Spencer style, with no option but to grit your teeth and wait for the pain…the bloke in the bike shop did tell me that it happened to everyone at least once but of course I'm not your average cyclist, I'm not that stupid!

Well it did happen…luckily, I'd pulled up outside a friend's house on a quiet estate…and forgot…and over I went with the usual result of very minor pain from a few cuts and bruises but a major hit to the pride…especially as there were two nine-year-olds walking up the path who p****d themselves laughing and thought it was so funny, they ran back to tell their dad. All while I was trying to look cool as though this was the way us advanced cyclists always dismounted.

So back to the helmet. No, I don't think it will do any good under an 18-ton truck but it might save me a headache when I forget again and sustain a minor bump to the head. I'm trying to cut down on weight so a pack of Nurofen is the last thing I need to be taking!

BB – *Love the writing style Ian, not something we've had too much exposure to in doing business with you! We'll be most impressed if you are able to continue to be as entertaining by day 10 though you will have all day to work on your composition, won't you. Maybe we should score the daily blog entries for entertainment value and gear our sponsorship to that. On the other hand, that might allow you to give up the physical bit by Bodmin and concentrate on creating entertaining little daily gems for the blog all wholly imaginary, of course. Do they fly from Exeter to John O'Groats by the way? Pity if you'd have to complete the job by cycling from Wick!*

Chapter 3
Day 2 – Oh What Fun We've Had

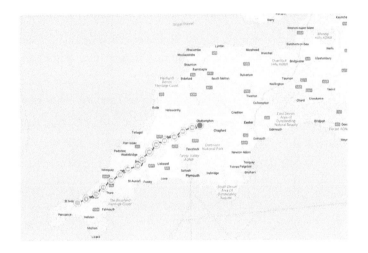

What a fun day we've had today!

Interesting to say the least, but the end result is that I'm in Sourton Cross in one piece if a little knackered.

I left Hayle about 8.45 am which was a bit later than I'd planned, but it took me longer than I thought to have breakfast and get creamed up (that's sun cream, including on my hair, but yes, the bum cream made its debut as well).

And it was hilly, very hilly, in fact looking at the stats on 'mapmyride', I think today is the hilliest of them all, nearly

4000 feet of climbs and I ended up about 900 feet higher than I started.

After about 20 miles, I was planning on a stop, but just couldn't find anywhere to do so. I was knackered, my bum was hurting (not chaffing, just felt a bit bruised) and I started to feel really down and thinking I had definitely bitten off more than I could chew. I finally found a McDonald's at 27 miles and stopped. I Found a table with a plug, got a cup of tea and three chicken selects and started to write down the rest of my route.

Because, remember that old fashioned nerd from the train with his paper maps compared to my snazzy iPhone app?

Well, I bet when he looked at his for directions it wasn't blank because there was no mobile phone or data signal...and I bet it didn't run out of battery either...I've spent so much time today stopping in various locations to try and get a signal that the first thing I did when I got to the hotel was nip next door for a massive map!

Lesson learnt.

Next leg was a quick 13 miles to Bodmin. Well, not that quick, but I didn't want to do any more because I knew my battery would need recharging and there is nowhere else for miles.

I had a quick panini and coffee in Bodmin before setting off armed with a nifty little short cut that took a big corner off the A30. So nifty in fact that it came back on the wrong side of the dual carriageway with barriers down the middle so there was no chance of me getting across to the way I wanted to go. There was, however, a bridge over the dual carriageway...straight in to a farmer's field!

So here's the choices:

a) Go back the way I've just come from for God knows how many miles and take the proper road.
b) Traipse down the farmers field for about half a mile to where it meets the A30 in the right direction.

The latter being the chosen option. So I get to a flattish bit of the field with just a chest high wooden fence and a bit of grassy stuff between me and the A30. I take the bag off the bike, climb over the fence and jump down ready to pull the bike over behind me…knee-deep in to muddy bloody water…the grass was hiding a marshy stream-like thing!

Several expletives later I'm back in the field moving further on to where it might be easier to get over…until the stream turns 90 degrees straight in front of me. Brilliant!

Now I wasn't in the scouts for nothing (actually it was the air cadets but it's practicality the same). I go back to my original crossing point and using a bit of fence that was practically hanging off I build myself a bridge over the stream. It's not as grand as the Humber bridge but it did the job and I'm back on the A30 in the right direction.

Feeling really good about my ingenuity, I plough on to my next stop at 62 miles – Launceston (does anyone know how to pronounce that?) and start to feel really fit and healthy.

However, at 70 miles, I've no idea where I am because the iPhone has died completely and the iPad can't get a signal – great…so I stay on the A30 and hope for the best. The last two miles before the hotel are all uphill and on finally arriving, I feel like my thighs are going to explode.

My back aches a bit as well. There's some strange twinge in my right thumb and my bum is very very bruised, although that pain seems to come and go. Very strange. Does anyone know if fat can get bruised, because if not, then I've got very serious problems!

At dinner time I happened to notice there was a horse running in the 3.35 at Redcar – Collateral Damage was its name and so I had a small wager. That might give you a small clue how certain parts of my anatomy are feeling after 30 miles of Cornish hills this morning!

It came seventh.

I went to buy a map and tea at the little chef attached to the hotel (there is nowhere else for miles). The tomato soup came and went back to be warmed up. Lasagne came and was OK for the first centimetre around the edge but then was frozen in the middle! Tea abandoned and off to bed although it's probably an appropriate time to publish part of my manifesto should I ever become involved in politics.

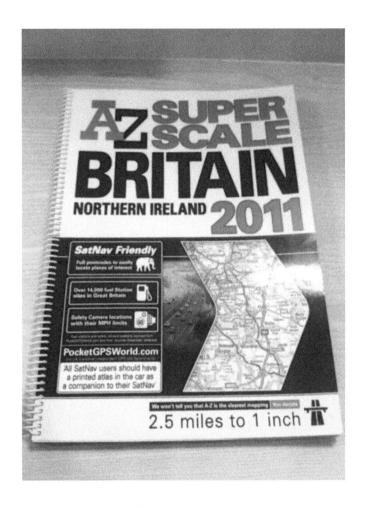

Today's purchase!

When I am Prime Minister

Cornwall wants independence…? Don't worry, it's first on the list of things to do.

You can keep your stupid black and white flag and your ridiculous own language (I can't believe we have to do dual signage in Cornwall like we do in Wales, there can't be more than five people who speak it). And have your coronary inducing pasties, cream teas, tin mines and your lack of mobile and 3G or 4G signal – any 'G' in fact (not that you'll know what that is). You can keep your daft shortcuts that end up in farmers' fields complete with hidden ditches full of muddy water…but most of all, you can keep your hills, every single one of them…no wonder you haven't got a professional football team, where would they play…? There's not a flat piece of ground anywhere.

PW – Lorn sten is how it's pronounced and Cornwall is my favourite place in the world……it's just that you've gone through the middle, rather than around the outside!!!

My Reply – Well you can be first minister when it's independent then P……and they'll be more edges to it when I've arranged for it to be cut off and floated in to the Atlantic!

JS – wow, what a day you had!

CH – Absolutely brilliant. You may know that I love that part of the world and it pleases me that you both got on so well. 'Lornston' is I think the correct pronunciation and I could have recommended a top pub if I'd known!

My Reply – I would have had a nice cream tea but Independent places seem to be a thing of the past, especially in a morning and after 5 pm…plus there's no Internet connection or the like to look anywhere up!

Chapter 4
How Did It Come to This?

So I am 95 miles into the ride and so far so good (ish), apart from dodgy shortcuts, hidden rivers, cold lasagne, no mobile signal, iPhones that drink battery life and a few other minor annoying things, all is going to plan. But how exactly did I get myself into this?

It was half past 9 on a wet miserable October Sunday morning. I'd got up, walked around the corner and bought myself the Sunday Times. It was either that or the Sunday People, which if I'm honest is more my kind of paper. You can read it from front to back in an hour and get a good grasp of what's happening in the world with plenty of pictures to back up the story. I say front to back, as any sports fan will testify, the correct order is to start on the back page and go back to where the adverts for stairlifts and hearing aids start and then flip to the front and go forward from there.

Anyway, it was the Times that got my vote, mainly because it had that many supplements that it would give me something to read for the whole day, which, when you are stuck in a two-bedroomed ground floor flat with just the tele for company is a big plus. I was looking out of the window, through the rain, at the big golden arches and wondering if I could justify a fifth McDonald's breakfast that week. To be fair, it would be one less than the week before and at six stone overweight, cutting back could only be good for me...so I put on my waterproof golf jacket, dashed across the road (as quick as an 18 stone bloke can dash!) – jumped over the wall (see previous comments) and ordered a double sausage and egg McMuffin with three hash browns...to take away.

10 minutes later I'm sat back at the window multitasking as only men can...hash brown in one hand, flicking through the paper with the other, when I came across an article by a travel writer who had just cycled from Lands End to John O'Groats or completed "LEJOG" as the cyclists call it. It's the best part of 900 miles and he was saying that for all that us Brits travel the globe to visit beauty spots and see brilliant scenery, that there is nothing more beautiful than this small island if you took the time to look.

I drive in the region of 30,000 miles a year around the UK for my job, but the vast majority of it is on soulless motorways and spent looking at the brake lights of the car in front so that as soon as they brake, I can as well, and don't plough in to the back of them. I learnt this lesson in my early 20s when I was driving past the Kop at Hillsborough during the time they were extending it and putting a roof on. Obviously I was checking on progress whilst unbeknown to me the lady in front had made the bizarre decision to pay more attention to the colour of the traffic lights and had come to a stop. The more I read the article, the more an idea started to form in my head.

I'd just turned 40-ish, OK 45, and was surely due a mid-life crisis. I'd always promised myself a tattoo, a motorbike and a blonde bimbo. However, on reflection, I decided that a motorbike would probably end up killing me and the wife told me a tattoo would result in a divorce. I was pondering the blonde bimbo but decided that would probably lead to both a divorce and being killed, by either the bimbo or the wife and so I decided there and then to do LEJOG as my mid-life crisis.

It probably says a lot about my mindset at that time that I'd had one a few months earlier which was why I was sitting in the flat with the TV whilst my son and wife were both in our home two miles away!

My mind was now moving full steam ahead. June would be the best time to do it with the long days, obviously I'd have plenty of holiday to burn and so I could book a couple of weeks off work and crack this. Nine months of training on a bike which wasn't in my possession at this point would solve the six stone excess baggage problem and I announced my intention to the world on Facebook.

A few people wanted to join me either in cycling or supporting and suffice to say, nine months later they were nowhere to be seen! So I did it on my own, me, my bike, a few provisions and off I went on 6 June, hopefully ending on 18 June.

AL – *You're bloody mental.*

Chapter 5
Day 3 Completed – Just!

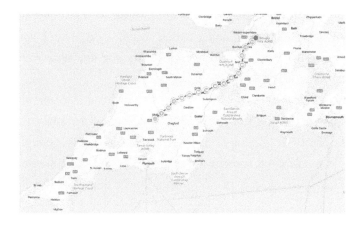

Not sure how to describe Day 3 other than "mixed".

How can anyone manage to set the alarm for 6 am and not get out of the hotel until 9…? I could understand it if I was a woman…I suppose snoozing for 18 minutes didn't help (today's challenge – why do snoozes generally last nine minutes on an alarm…why not 10?)

I had a warm bath and then decided to take up Mr K's idea of an ice bath…obviously not ice but I drained all the hot water out and filled it with cold…sat in there for a few minutes and then had a hot shower, shave etc.

I then had a breakfast of omelette and hash browns with some jam on toast which took longer than usual as I was busy transferring today's route off the iPad and on to paper. I also ripped out all the pages from the atlas that I'll need and ditched the rest.

Surprisingly, the first 10 miles went really well, helped by the fact that there was a lot of downhills and I felt really good. But then payback time arrived for those downhills and for the next 15 miles there were lots and lots of uphills with seemingly a lot less downhills. But I didn't feel anywhere near as low as I did at this stage yesterday. This morning's route was more village to village than main road and as such once again there was nowhere to stop until three hours had passed.

At which point I found a pub called the Black Dog, in a little village of the same name. Homemade fish pie with broccoli and cauliflower (yes, I had both!) was the dinner of choice and Dave, the barman, who was a friendly chap tells me that from here to Tiverton is a lot flatter and a lot more downhills so I can't wait to set off again.

I had dinner with five old dears (more on this in a bit) and set off for Tiverton. Dave turned out to be a liar, either that or I took a wrong turning somewhere (I know I definitely took one) and to cut a long story short, after lots of looking at maps and apps turning this way and that, I finally found the A38 and got to Tiverton about half 3 and stopped for a coffee.

I just about managed to get a mobile signal and logged on to 'mapmyride'. Imagine my despair to discover that six and half hours after setting off, I was the grand total of 32 miles from my starting point. I nearly said covered 32 miles but I had definitely done more than that, a lot more. That one definite wrong turn was probably two, three or more…I was devastated…at this rate it would be midnight before I got to my hotel just south of Bristol.

Gee'd myself up with the idea that the delay was in looking at maps all the time and now I was on the A38, I would be a lot quicker and the last 20 miles would be flat.

I had a good run towards Taunton for the first five miles but then started to get twinges in my right knee (which I had checked a few months ago and the doc told me was just scar tissue and cycling would do it good). I was just starting to get worried about it when it seemed to go away, either that or the pain in my right thigh had taken over. A muscular pain just above the knee and I knew if I wasn't careful, I could do some damage, so I had to nurse it through all the way to Bristol by applying most of the force with my left leg and using lower gears.

Hours and miles behind schedule, lucky to get to the hotel before dark and a knackered right thigh…fantastic!!!

But, I got to Taunton, had a quick break and then the last 27 miles…they were flat…very very flat…and you know how I had a rant about the hills of Cornwall on day two, well flat's not good either…at least with hills you get chance to take your bum off the seat (both up and down hill). But flat doesn't allow that, it's just backside in the seat and pedal…and pedal, and pedal…for mile after mile after mile…anyway, I finally arrived at my hotel (at the top of a steep hill!) at 9.40 pm and with no lights, that was cutting it fine.

Seeing as I had passed through Taunton, I had another small wager on a horse called "Botham" in the 9 o'clock at

Hamilton. For the non-sporting folk out there, Sir Ian Botham, probably the best cricketer in my lifetime so far, played for many years for Somerset whose main ground was in Taunton. You can find out if it did any better than yesterday's in the comments below!

Bath, shower, bed!

Oh, and I nearly forgot…lunch…five old dears who are having their weekly luncheon and are fascinated to find someone in the pub who they've never seen before.

"Come and tell us all about yourself and what you are doing here, dear," they demanded.

Half an hour later I've nodded lots and hardly said a word but Chrissie's sister has had a fall in the conservatory and broken her arm and foot…Pauline has finally sold her house but they want to move in by August and Doreen is telling her to be firm and "absolutely tell them you cannot possibly move out by August and to go and look somewhere else if they are in a rush…" Just the sort of advice you want to be getting in the sort of housing climate where buyers are king and your house has been for sale for two years!

And then, out of nowhere, Rhona, who must be 70 odd, asks me what network my mobile is with…apparently O2 is just about OK but orange and T Mobile haven't been working since 28 April and it's a disgrace…all the others just look at her like she's some sort of freak talking about mobile networks at her age.

So I get up and make my excuses despite their protests that I should have a stiff one for the road!

Oh, and Linda…sat in the corner knitting the whole time and knocked back three whiskies while I was there!

AB – Ha so funny! Love it! You must have looked like a Pimp out with his Bitches!!! Which one did you give a 'backie' home???

PS. Linda sounds a lot like the old me!!! Obviously I've given up knitting.

And if you set your alarm to go off at 8.00 am, hitting snooze will make it go off again at 8.10 am. The 9 minutes is because by the time you hit the button there is less than 10 minutes until it goes off again. It will be 9 minutes something depending on how long you take to press snooze. That is why.

My Reply – You may be good at poetry, but you are talking rubbish about this. If I hammer snooze at 8 am it goes off again at 8.09!

LJ – Well, I've took a lunch break today (very unusual for me, as you know how busy we are in Commercial ;o)) and decided to see if you had kept to your word and updated us on your experiences this week.1 hour later (ish, don't grass me up to the boss!), a number of hankies and some very strange looks from the people around me, I've finish reading!

Sounds like you're having a lot of fun! and I'm wondering if you're taking it seriously enough. Hee Hee! ;o)

Looking forward to what challenges you have face today.

My Reply – Fun!.... Fun?.... you are joking right?... some people might like their backsides feeling like this but it's not my idea of fun I can tell you!

ST – *looks like Botham couldn't be bothered – hope you're not feeling the same. Well done Ian keep going but watch out for Bristol it's busier than you might think!*

SJ – *Just think of all the people you wouldn't have met Ian if you hadn't entertained doing this xxx*

And just a thought but wouldn't it have been much easier (and far less painful) to just bet on the horses to try and raise money instead of cavorting in muddy fields with a bike on your bike??

That said, you're doing brill keep up the good work xxx

My Reply – *What do you think?…Yesterday's horse came 7th and ST has said above how well todays did. If I was any good at the horse game I'd have been sat on a beach in Barbados many years ago!*

Chapter 6
Jesus, the Missing Years

What I've learned over the last few months or so is that cycling gives you plenty of time to think…and one thing I have been thinking about is, what exactly did Jesus get up to between being born in a stable in a hail of publicity, up until he appeared again at about 33 complete with a beard and an NVQ in carpentry?

What did he do at school? Did he have meetings with the careers teacher who would tear his hair out at hearing the young Jesus say for the millionth time, "I don't need to do algebra, I'm going to be a Messiah,"…was he called "Christ" at school like I was called "Jenkins", or was Jesus his full and only name like Pele?

And what about Mum and Dad, what happened to them…? Could Joseph and Mary pack in work once they realised Jesus had special talents, knowing that Jesus would set them up with a nice pad…? And how old were they when they died…? To be honest, if I was Jesus's dad, I'd be pretty hacked off if I wasn't still alive today… What's the point on having a son who could make anything happen if you get run over by a donkey aged 52?

And the teenage Jesus…what was he like…when Mary opened up with, "Jesus, don't for one minute think you are going out around Bethlehem with those 12 mates of yours until that stable is tidied up." Did Jesus respond with, "OMG, Mum, do I have to do everything around here?" before slamming the stable door and sweeping the 1500 loaves of bread off the table that he'd just made?

Now some of these answers may be in the Bible, but to be honest, I had to jettison three of my mars bars from my bag before I set off, due to lack of room, so the Bible definitely had to stay at home as well…so over to you lot (JS) for some answers.

And answers I got. As expected from JS, as she is the most religious person I know. What I wasn't expecting was answers from SM. We had known each other since school and to say I was surprised at her answer would be a massive understatement.

The way the answers descended from a religious conversation to rude poetry was, however, no surprise at all!

JA – I think you have had too much time alone Ian. The concern I had for your physical wellbeing as you start your journey has now changed into concern for your mental wellbeing.

SJ – I soooo can't wait for Julie's answer it should make for interesting reading! Oh, and by the way JA, I've been concerned for his mental wellbeing for a long time!

CH – Me and B are. Cyclists that is. We go to Bradfield. And back. We're even talking about going around Derwent including a bacon sarnie somewhere along the route.

Talking of routes, I've just had a look at yours and for once, I am full of admiration. And yes, I'll admit it, disbelief. Hope it goes well, and I'll watch this blog thing with interest. Can't help thinking you'll need a rest day though.

By the way Jesus isn't real.

JS (prepare yourselves) *– Ian, huge blessings to you honey as you set off for your adventure. I'm so proud of you Mr J! You made me smile with the blog and indeed it provides very interesting questions.*

An accurate reply requires a certain amount of time and I know not all the answers at present so I need to seek advice too and I am facing the half hour mad rush before school, so I will return with a more detailed response later. However, to sum up my own thoughts. Jesus did come to live on earth in human form. He faced all the same highs and lows that we do, all the temptations and frustrations whilst living as a Jew under the dictatorship of the Roman leaders. His immaculate conception led his mother and father to be aware of who He was to the world, though they parented just as we do, but I would imagine that as He got older God directed them to allow Jesus to live as 'normal' as possible. The plan for Jesus' life was ordained by God himself, as ours is, but you are right, what fascinating thinking and I will definitely be researching it further.

What makes me feel very comforted Ian is that you even consider these questions. God loves you so much and there is nothing that you could do that would make Him love you any more or any less. He sent His only son to die for you, to rise and offer you eternal life, so your interest in the practical side of Jesus' life and ministry is totally understandable.

As you cycle through the green, green valleys and along the urban highways just remember that back home we are all so proud of you: your family, your friends and your God! Use this time to consider areas of faith that make you ponder and await hopefully an accurate response from me that we can discuss further. Huge hugs and take really really good care.... Bless ya...J x.

PS you are funny.

JS (researched response) – *Hello again. here is what I know so far. The Bible gives very little information of the growing up life of Jesus, but I have sought out some passages that provide a small insight.*

Firstly, like any other boy, He had to grow both physically and mentally. He probably went to school as almost all Jewish boys did in those days. As a boy He "grew in wisdom and stature, and in favour with God and men" (Luke 2:52). Secondly, as a boy Jesus grew spiritually and in His understanding of the Scriptures. At the age of 12, Jesus went to Jerusalem with His family and He became separated from them. When Mary and Joseph finally found Him, He was in the Temple, "sitting among the teachers, listening to them and asking them questions" (Luke 2:46). When they asked Him what He was doing, He replied, "Didn't you know I had to be in my Father's house?" (Luke 2:49). He had already realised He had a special relationship with God (How awesome a thought).

From there Ian it is presumed that Jesus followed the family line of carpentry, though translation suggests that

47

labourer is a more accurate interpretation. Little is known about this stage of His life and possibly those who documented it felt it was not necessary to record, or maybe further scrolls are out there to be discovered. There are theories that suggest He travelled to India and there is a website that tells a bit more about these if you want to know more.

As for when, how and where Joseph died, we again know very little, this reflects the lack of importance that the gospel writers placed on Joseph as they saw him only as Mary's husband rather than Jesus' father. Jesus' Father was God.

Hope this helps a bit...lol.

I was thinking that you could maybe put up a poetry blog if you're inspired by anything you see on your travels (apart from totty) What do you think?

I would love to read some!

Bye 4 now.

My Reply – *So in a nutshell he did a runner from home at 12, ran off to the circus in India where he did menial labouring jobs and came back pretending he was a skilled carpenter. No one gives one about Mum and Dad and although God loves me, He's a He...just my luck!!!*

And Poetry might be a good idea... I might do it on a local theme each day, for example.

"there was a young woman in Bude..."

Leave it with me.

JA – *Can't we all help with the poetry?*
There was a young woman in Bude
Who found cyclists incredibly rude.

JS – *they would whistle and stare*
as she waved her legs in the air….

JA – *(who by now is obsessed with the poetry)*
There was a young woman in Bude
Who found cyclists incredibly rude
they would whistle and stare
as she waved her legs in the air
And laid on the road in the nude.

SM – *I don't know who Julie is, but I feel a kinship…your contemplating God, even if it is in the physical practicalities of his life is profound…. As you cycle along your route, everything you see is touched by the hand of God. As the sun shines on your face, feel his warmth shining on you…. Sending you love and light to speed you on your way. Sxxx*

Meanwhile B has lifted his head from the sand and is now on the 3rd verse of there was a young woman from Bude….

My Reply to all – *Right, a few things to put straight.*

First off, just because I asked what happened to Jesus in his teenage years does not mean I have turned to God…I have no desire to take on the vicar's role in Emmerdale and will continue to use his, sorry His, name in vain especially now you've told me I can't do anything to upset Him.

Secondly, I am not a bloody cyclist……I'm just a bloke who, as a one off, is riding a bike for a few days…after that I will be back in my gas guzzling, environment destroying car, cursing cyclists for getting in my way and riding side by side.

***SJ** – Oh Ian just as it was going so well you've had to let yourself down! Both Susan & Julie were feeling love & compassion for you. They thought you were a kindred spirit. Oh well, onwards & upwards. Can't wait to hear B's rhyme about the ladies of Bude lol xx*

Chapter 7
Day 4 – Best Day So Far

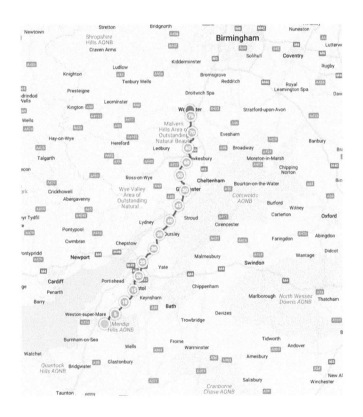

To say I'm feeling a hundred times better tonight than last night would be a massive understatement (in which case why don't I just say I feel a thousand times better?) Anyway,

I set the alarm for 6 am again, battled with snooze for 18 minutes, binned having a shave, had breakfast and then planned the route as follows;

Get on A38 and pedal until Worcester.

Sounds boring but it beats faffing around with all those maps and country lanes and wrong turns.

I decided that I need to be more realistic with my times and that my original 10mph is a bit hard given I've got 16kg of weight on the back, not to mention 109 on the saddle! So I set today's 75 miles in to five lots of 15-mile stints, each taking two hours (7.5mph) and I would stop every 15 miles for 30 min and 60 min breaks in turn.

I set off just before 8 am (still some work to be done on reducing the alarm to leaving time") north towards Bristol airport and Bristol itself. The 'mapmyride' app that I am using shows me all the elevations on the routes and also labels any major hills which are graded 1–5 with 1 being the hardest and 5 still bloody steep and long (for those who know it, slack hill on the way from Chesterfield to Matlock is "only" a grade 5!)

My day in Cornwall had 9 x grade 5 hills, yesterday had 6 x grade 5's and today only had 1 climb…five miles after I'd set off and it was a grade 4…up the hill towards the airport but well worth it for the views of the Clifton suspension bridge and Bristol itself with it's funny multi coloured houses and the ride down the other side was good too!

Just into Bristol itself and 15 miles is up so I call in Sainsburys for a cuppa and a flapjack before setting off through Bristol…which despite having some, let's call them lively, football fans spanning both clubs, I quite like. I took a scenic cycling route which went past Ashton Gate, the home of Bristol City and on a riverside path in to the city centre that I've walked many times on visiting the ground. I then left Bristol past the Italian restaurant and coffee lounge where Ben, AL, JL and myself ended up before a match against Bristol Rovers a few seasons ago when we couldn't get in any pubs.

17 miles later, at half 12, I stop at a pub for a fantastic homemade lasagne…and take note eateries of the world, this is how this type of conversation should go.

Me: "Can I have lasagne please but without the garlic bread or salad?"

Very pretty barmaid: "If you don't want salad and garlic bread, it will be a bit empty so shall I get them to put you some chips on instead at no extra cost?"

Is the Pope Catholic?

Oh, and the softest of sofa's to sit on as well…this is just ideal!

How comfy does this look – and it was!

Polish that off and tootle off to Gloucester and I can't believe how good I feel and I am really enjoying myself.

A cup of tea in Gloucester and just 25 miles left. I get to Tewksbury in 10 miles which looks a nice place and I really should have stopped there but I decided to carry on for another five. And then decided that as there is only 10 miles left, I might as well carry on. To quote Julia Roberts in *Pretty Woman,* "Big mistake. Big. Huge," and I hit the wall. The last 10 miles took me nearly two hours, not helped by having to have frequent time outs to stop the pain in my bum making me pass out or be sick.

But all in all a good day. I arrived in Worcester at just gone 7 pm and am just tucking into a sloppy Giuseppe's in Pizza Express.

The thigh is much better today, (although I have to be careful not to set off with that leg from junctions) but the third finger on my right hand and ball of my left hand are still numb and tingling, presumably from holding the handlebars…and then there's the bottom area!

I don't think it could be more painful…I'm hoping that it will just go very numb as soon as possible so that I can't feel it anymore or that I'll get used to it but at the moment I feel like walking in to A&E and just asking them if they can stick a needle in it, that will stop the pain.

However, not content with using a bit of fence to build myself a bridge over the stream on day two, today I have come up with an even better idea.

Ice is supposed to help injured areas, yes? – but the Travelodge in Worcester doesn't do ice of any sort and I got here too late to go to Boots for an ice pack.

And as you know, my backside really could do with an ice pack.

However, there is a vending machine in the reception area that sells "ice cold drinks".

Ice cold...as in an ice pack in a can almost...£2 later (robbing sods) and I'm sitting with a can of diet coke (unopened) up my crack and everyone's happy!

Genius or what?

The only thing is that it's warm now so I'll have to chuck it away as there's no fridge.

88 miles on tomorrow's leg so an early night will be in order.

AB – *No offence Ian but rather be me than your can of coke.*

JS – *You're doing fab hon, are you taking lots of pics along the way? Loving the fact that you chose the DIET variety of coke, At least you didn't go for 7UP!*

AL – *Glad to hear you had a better day yesterday bloke. I was beginning to think you wouldn't make it past Bristol. I've been reading the blog with interest as the updates get sent straight to my Blackberry. However, it's a nightmare trying to reply. I was going to try and get across to Knutsford tonight for a pint or two, but I've got to go south on business and need to get back to be a taxi for the kids. You'll be in Scotland before I'm free at this rate!*

Enjoy tomorrow's 88 miles and don't forget to take that coke can out of your a**e before you start pedalling!

All the best.

Chapter 8
Poetry

You will have seen in chapter six how my slightly irreverent question regarding Jesus somehow ended up with a request for poetry with the first example ending up exactly where I expected. However, I thought I'd persevere and see where it went so each day I would post the first line of a poem, loosely based on the route I was taking that day. These are the results!

First off, a few ground rules.

1. Poems rhyme. It's not up for debate and all you airy fairy, arty educated types who are now in the teaching profession (you know who you are!) can forget about trying to tell me otherwise. If it doesn't rhyme, then it's just a paragraph or a very short story.
2. Each day's poem must be local to where I am…you can either wait for my first line or have a look on the map and make up your own.

Here's my first attempt:

(Bude)
There was a young woman from Bude
Who asked me to do things that were rude
She made my body start to tingle
But I said, "Sorry, love, I'm not single."
And went instead for some food

There is an alternative version to this but seeing as my wife is reading, then I'll have to stick with this one!

A collaboration of JA and JS

There was a young woman in Bude
Who found cyclists incredibly rude
they would whistle and stare
as she waved her legs in the air
And laid on the road in the nude.

AB –
There was a young woman from Bude
Who asked you to do something rude
You said well I might…
Well go on then alright
And now S is in a terribly bad mood!!!

My reply – Only because you've told her!!!… I'd prefer it if she believed mine

AW –
There was an old man from Hayle
He really was rather pale.

He liked fish and chips
and his wife had big T**s
Oh what a peculiar tale!!!

My reply – I like this one, especially the fact that you've given "T**s" a capital T a bit like religious people use a capital H when using He and His to describe God....obviously showing what you worship – which I can't fault!!!

Only thing is, and I might be being pedantic...does "chips" and "t**s" rhyme?

AB –

There was a tough ride named LEJOG
That was described day by day in a blog
By a bloke with a cycle
Who's friends took the Michael
When he gets back they'll all be agog!

JS –

There is a man who has a bike,
who is very funny and you can't help like.
He cycles from THERE,
to all the way HERE,
let's hear it for Jenkie and give a big cheer!

Me –

There was an old man from Newquay
Who married a tasty young bird called Dee
She wasn't one for long talks
But boy did she have good n***s

And often had em out for all to see
AB –
There was an old bloke in Newquay
Who got stung on the arse by a bee?
'Ouch' he said with a frown
'Cos he couldn't sit down
and had to push and not peddle on day 3

My reply – I've no idea what you do for a job but it's the wrong one…never knew you were so rhythmical!!!

AW –
There was an old man from Newquay
His best mate was a trannie called Suki
She wore polka dots tights
and smoked Marlborough lights
and had a pet snake called Spooky!

SJ –
There was an old woman from Devon
who thought oh my god I'm in heaven
as she saw the cream buns
but she stuck to her guns
and said no way can I manage all seven

I did originally do a rather more rude version but thought
I ought to change it…. didn't want to offend lol xx

JA –
There was an old woman from Devon
Who died & did get to heaven

At the gate was St Pete

She thought it seemed neat

There were even some clouds to tread on

We're back to religion again!

JS –

There was a young woman from Devon,

who had not been kissed since she was seven

Dry was her mouth,

and as for down south…

let's hope there is KY in heaven.

PW –

There was an old woman from Devon

Who'd just died aged 77.

Cause of death you'll not like,

She fell off her old bike.

Now she's with her old man in heaven!

Boom, Boom!

AW's reply – I didn't know Basil Brush had entered the mix! LOL Ax

AB –

There was a young couple from Devon

And their names were Tracy and Kevin

She was always a tease

When she got down on her knees

She prayed for Kevin to get into Heaven!!!

AB –

There once was a pub called 'The Black Dog'
Which was mentioned one day in a blog
The landlord Dave was a liar
And dropped Ian in the mire
Oh the traumas of cycling LEJOG!
While there Ian ordered some lunch
On broccoli and cauliflower he munched
The fish pie he reminisced
Of something he missed
But he'd get some back home was his hunch

In the pub five old ladies were frisky
One of whom like to knit and drink whiskey
Another one she advised
on mobile Networks, Ian surmised
He should drink up and leave there quite briskly.

B –

There was a young lady from Ripple
Who suffered from jogger's nipple
Her husband did laugh
When he saw her in the bath
Treating it with raspberry ripple

And I was expecting a Bristol theme yesterday so you can have it anyway.

There was a young woman from Bristol
Her bosom was rather a fistful
Her boyfriend from Devon

Thought he was in heaven
What went through his head was just wishful

It appears that I've overcome my writer's block.

There was a young man with writers block, so instead he decided to play with his...anyway back to Bristol.

JA –
There was a young lady from Ripple
Who would always have a daily tipple
She used to drink brandy
But it made her feel randy
And go rather erect in the nipple

Me – (those who don't know football and Sheffield football in particular won't understand)

"Micky Adams came home from Stoke on Trent
And very soon brought in Marcus Bent
Don't worry my dears
He hasn't scored for two years
Our relegation chances he won't dent".
And he didn't!!!

JA –
There was a man from Stoke on Trent
Who bought a second-hand tent
He knew it was a pup
Cos he couldn't get it up
And found his pole was bent

CP –

There was a Nissan driver from Preston
Who struggled whilst putting his vest on
He fell down the stair
Broke bones by the pair
That silly old driver from Preston

My wife's support at my own poetry efforts can best be summed up with the following comment she made;

SJ –

I'm sure that people will be delighted to read your entries into the poetry competition but what they really want to know is how you got on each day. Can you leave the poetry to us and concentrate on updating us of any mishaps, old ladies in pubs, muddy fields etc. We await with baited breath for each days account of your journey xx

At this point in proceedings, Sunday was a mere sleep away and therefore in line with a very sensible request from one of my religious guru's (I only had one before this trip now I've got a Derbyshire and Yorkshire version), with tomorrow being Sunday, we will suspend the poetry competition (seeing as you have all got gutter brains). Instead, we will have a deep and meaningful conversation about a religious type topic that I will post on the day.

Chapter 9
Day 5 – The Longest One

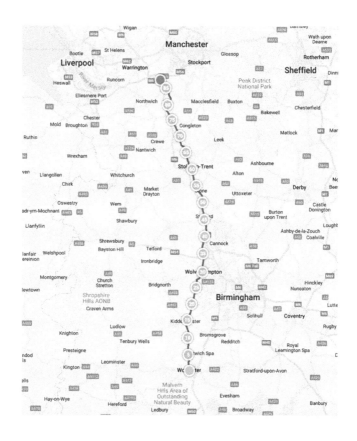

Worcester to Knutsford today. Again, a fairly flat run and
about 89 miles which is my longest planned day of the trip,

although I suspect the actual mileage on day three has already beaten that!

The route goes through the likes of Kidderminster, Wolverhampton and Stafford in the morning followed by some of the smaller Cheshire villages in the afternoon. Holmes Chapel to name but one which I remember visiting during my days as a spectacle frame salesman.

I stuck fairly rigidly to stopping every 15 miles so that I didn't blow up and struggle at the end, even so, the last 10 miles were hard work.

Today, completely out of the blue, somewhere around Dudley, I came across a field. Now a field in or around the Black Country is one thing but this was no ordinary field and I imagine it's exactly the kind of thing the journalist that inspired me to do the ride must have been talking about. This was a full-on poppy field which you'd expect to see in Flanders. I was awestruck and had to stop for a few minutes to take in the beauty and surprise of it all.

The poppy field of Dudley

Further good news is that the diet coke seemed to be working its magic and if the pain in my backside was 9/10 yesterday (with 0 being the usual day to day pain on a day not following a curry), then today it was down to about 6. I'm pretty sure it was the coke that did it, although I did wear two pairs of padded shorts for the first time and take an accidental overdose of ibuprofen, so they could have helped a bit as well.

However...and it's a big however...the bum pain has now been overtaken by GN...genital numbness is the medical term I believe and all I can say is that it's like having freezing cold water constantly running over the old chaps...sounds like it might not be too bad but after eight hours, it's no fun, believe me.

When it first came on, I thought it was just cold air that was blowing around there so in another moment of ingenuity (I should be a field surgeon for the army!), I stopped and used my bandana as a makeshift "warmer" for the area...it made no difference at all!

Genital numbness pain rating for yesterday was 7!

I think I've finally cracked the issue of getting out of the hotel within two hours of the alarm going off. I was out and on the road for 7 am today, getting a few hours riding in before I stopped for 20 minutes or so as the Managing Director of the company I work for asked me to take five minutes of his audio conference with the sales team to update everyone on where I was, raise the profile of the charities and a few words on what motivated me. What I hadn't realised at this point was that my daily blog was attracting nearly 500 views a day, mainly from work colleagues...There was a definite surge of donations on the day so a big thank you was deserved for GW, the MD and DL my immediate manager for sorting that out for me.

As I said it was a long run and I arrived at the Premier Inn at Mere for about 9 o'clock, had a cold bath, a hot shower, a hot bath and off to bed.

In summary; Bum better, other things around that area, a lot worse!

And as I've not had a dilemma since setting off, here's one for everyone to ponder:

Hannah Spearitt or Rachel Stevens?

CH – From that, do I presume you are suffering from what I call tingle cock? By that I don't mean I'm referring to you as 'cock' like I'm from Barnsley, and the condition as 'tingle', but the tingling, numbing sensation you get when you've been cycling for a while. Or is there only me gets that?

My Reply – it's my balls…like they are constantly under running cold water…it's not nice!

SM – You do realise this poetry lark is taking over my hubbies' life, just don't get onto anything lavatorial because there really will be only one winner!

It's really good you are all talking regularly. Is this like man therapy? If so, can you talk about something deep and meaningful for me? Ta xx

PB – Told you about GN didn't I! It may have "benefits" when the trip is over though!!!

(I'm not aware that any "benefits" were forthcoming unless I completely misread what PB meant!)

SJ – *Hmmm not really a dilemma as much as wishful thinking but I thought you had a definite preference for Hannah xx*

PM – *If it has to be one or the other give me Rachael every time. I knew you'd quickly find a subject I could comment on!*

AL – *Rachel Stevens – defo.*

CH – *Was Stevens, but latterly Spearitt even if she has got an interesting accent.*

Chapter 10
Salad Dodgers Of the
World Rejoice

Around the time of my journey, news broke of an E. coli outbreak in the UK. Now some people who know me may have noticed (many have even taken the time to kindly comment as such) but me and Salad aren't exactly big mates. In fact, it's fair to say that I've had very little salad since I was er…well ever, although I can't remember my very early years. But I can guarantee that for as long as I can remember, tomatoes, cucumber, radish's etc have been well off the menu. Occasionally if I can't be bothered to wait 40 minutes for them to cook a new one without, then I may just tolerate the shreds of lettuce on a big mac (but the gherkin always gets binned!) but that's my limit.

And over the years I've had plenty of advice about what a poor diet I have…wives, girlfriends (before I was married SJ!), doctors, nurses, friends (apparently!) and even a nutritionist have all told me I need to eat more salad.

So imagine my surprise, nay delight, to hear about the cause of the E. coli outbreak currently sweeping Europe.

Let's do a group exercise at this stage, all open up a new window and Google "cause of E. coli"…15 million plus results in about this number.

13 million – Cucumber

1 million – Tomatoes

1 million – Salad of any sort

0 – Chips, chicken kebab and mushy peas.

0 – Dominos large, thin crust pepperoni passion pizza, with extra cheese.

0 – Chips and cheese sauce with a half-pound cheeseburger.

0 – Chicken tikka masala, chips and a keema naan.

0 – Calzone

Now I know smugness isn't an attribute that we are supposed to aspire to, but bugger it, an occasional bout must be good for the soul!

Right, all that talk of food has made me hungry, I'm off for a kebab.

SJ – Wives?? Wives?? how many have you got??

BB – I have a certain fellow feeling with you on this one Ian, a hot pie has infinitely more salivatory appeal than the oft offered salad box. I think the bravery of "wives" deserves a big plus although I can think of less suicidal ways of introducing the topic! Probably a good job you're going to be away for a fortnight.

SJ – Luckily he's got an understanding wife Brian – that and the fact that there wouldn't be two of us mad enough to put up with him!

JA – *My salad dodging husband said the same – until I reminded him of mad cow disease & bird flu. Neither of which have put him off meat.*

Chapter 11
Day 6 – Cooking Bat

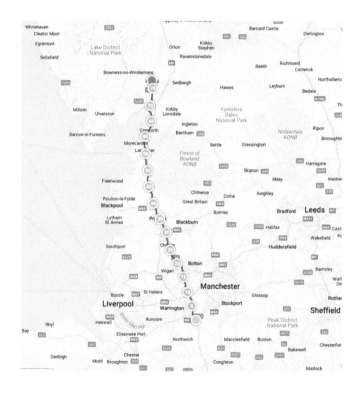

Well, I suppose the only surprise is that it took until Preston to happen, but I had my first "incident" today…only a minor one, but annoying all the same.

I was going through Preston and in a queue at the red lights I went down the inside of the traffic in the cycle lane. I went past a red Nissan who tried his best to pull in a bit to block me and pipped as I went past. Lights change to green and off we go, he passes me, pips again and gesticulates.

Unluckily for him, the next set of lights are only 200 yards away and they are at red so this time he pulls right over to the curb completely blocking the cycle lane so that I can't get past. Absolute moron. Not to be beaten I went around the back of him, down the outside of his car and back in to the cycle lane in front of him…he must have been livid!

Anyway, it turns out that I'd called that completely wrong and that he just wanted a chat because when he came past me again, he wound the window down (it might have been electric but "he pressed a button to decline the window" doesn't quite have the same ring to it!). The traffic noise was a bit loud but I'm sure he said he was cooking a bat? (Must be a local delicacy!) and also I think he told me that when he wasn't doing the cooking or driving his Nissan around Preston that he was a merchant banker…that's certainly what it sounded like.

Seeing as I couldn't hear him properly and I was intrigued to know whether you roasted or fried a bat, I invited him to pull over at the next opportunity and we could chat in more detail.

He decided that was a good idea and did so. As I approached his car in the layby he had pulled into, only one thing was going through my mind…I was repeating it to myself over and over… "Don't forget to take your feet out of the pedals, don't forget to take your feet out of the pedals"...however just as I did exactly that and pulled up behind him, he changed his mind and drove off again...I think the bat may have been burning!

Other than that, another interesting day...I missed a turning 300 yards after leaving the hotel and ended up taking a detour through Warrington, but once again I didn't encounter any rain. When I got to Lancaster, there was a canal path signposted for cyclists that went to Carnforth about six miles away. I did a quick check on the map which showed me that it was a bit further than sticking with the road but I reminded myself that this trip was about seeing the UK, not racing from A to B as quickly as possible and so I took to the canal path and was glad I did. It was a really nice scenic route with great views over the bay on the other side.

The first 25 miles were really hard, both mentally and physically. This came as a big surprise as I thought the day before would be a hard day given the distance it was, but I felt great when I had finished and expected things to just get better and easier from then on. I think the wrong turning right at the start of the day affected me mentally as I was thinking that every turn of the pedal is the one I didn't need to do if I'd gone the right way. I've also learnt that rather than having good days and bad days, it's more likely to be good and bad sessions, so just because it starts badly, needn't set the tone for the day...and later on in the morning I had a great run where I really felt fit and that I was making good progress.

Anyway, I'm over halfway now...another tough one tomorrow...best part of 90 miles including a grade 3 climb of over three miles long and 2 grade five climbs of over a mile…can't wait for the other side of them!

CH – *Sorry, but I find it really difficult to believe that you have only had the one 'incident' in around 400 miles!*
Maybe it is the soothing, calming effects of cycling that are lengthening your fuse, so to speak.

SJ – *Maybe he will come back a changed man CH!!!*

My Reply – *Maybe it's because I know to choose fights I can win…99% of the time if someone wants to pick a fight with my car they are going to lose…this week the boot is well and truly on the other foot!*

And anyway, who says I've got a short fuse!

AM – *Hi Ian, have just sat and read all of your blog and attached comments, now that hubby has forwarded the link to our home email! Not very often I read stuff that makes me lol, but sat with my glass of Pinot Grigio (or should I just have said "white wine" as they all taste the same!) reading this has got Saturday evening off to a good start. Keep up the good work and commiserations on the "bum" crisis!*
Love AM xx

My reply – *Glad you like it AM….and yes, white wine would have been fine. You know my views on wine. There is White and Red, they just put different labels on bottles to look posh but the stuff in the bottle is always the same. And that Rose stuff is just the two mixed up…you'll be telling me next that your car runs better on Esso unleaded than on Shell!*

Chapter 12
Sunday Reflection –
Moses V Jesus

So, Jesus and Moses is an interesting one. I'm not even sure they were about at the same time (R.E. was last thing on a Friday afternoon for me, so even on the days when I wasn't in the pub with AL recreating that week's Bullseye, the mind definitely was elsewhere) but if they were, what sort of relationship did they or would they have had?

I mean Moses must have been a bit miffed…there he goes just looking at the sea and he can do this magic trick to clear a path down the middle…very much the David Blaine of his time…and then along comes Jesus who makes him look like a kids' party entertainer with his bag of tricks including turning water to wine and his bread and fishes thing, not to mention his Easter spectacular!

So, was Moses jealous or did he and Jesus get on and swap notes…were they members of an early years magic circle and did they even know what each other got up to?

Over to you JS!

JS – *Hiya Ian, an interesting post again from you.*

Moses lived long before Jesus and it is written that he went to the Mount Nebo and lay down to sleep (die). Later in the New Testament it is written that Moses appeared with the disciples, talking with Jesus. Many Christians believe that Moses was raised by God from the dead to receive his place in heaven.

Moses is seen by many as a representative of the Old Testament. His restoration to the eternal life through Jesus gives hope and encouragement to those who feel all is too late.

The miracles that both Moses and Jesus provided come from the God of the heavens and earth and I would doubt that Jesus was fed up that Moses was able to do the things that he did, after all, parting the seas led the children of Israel to safety, and the rest is history. I also found the following and I think it is very clever. Funny, but on a serious note it depicts the important role that Moses had but also identifies the red tape society that we now all live in.

Moses was sitting in the Egyptian ghetto. Things were terrible. Pharaoh wouldn't even speak to him. The rest of the Israelites were mad at him and making the overseers even more irritable than usual. He was about ready to give up.

Suddenly a booming, sonorous voice spoke from above:

"You, Moses, heed me! I have good news, and bad news."

Moses was staggered. The voice continued:

"You, Moses, will lead the People of Israel from bondage. If Pharaoh refuses to release your bonds, I will smite Egypt with a rain of frogs".

"You, Moses, will lead the People of Israel to the Promised Land. If Pharaoh blocks your way, I will smite Egypt with a plague of Locust."

"You, Moses, will lead the People of Israel to freedom and safety. If Pharaoh's army pursues you, I will part the waters of the Red Sea to open your path to the Promised Land."

Moses was stunned. He stammered, "That's…. that's fantastic. I can't believe it! – But what's the bad news?"

"You, Moses, must write the Environmental Impact Statement."

Cycle safe and chat soon. x

MP – *Hi Ian, I hope you are having a nice Sunday! I've just had a full English, albeit only a small portion as we are having Sunday lunch and I can already smell the beef in the oven. The Yorkshire mix is just resting in the fridge whilst the Jersey royals are being gently scraped! Wondering whether to open a bottle of wine to sip whilst I browse the Sundays'.*

No maybe I shouldn't, I suddenly have this feeling of guilt thinking of you pushing forever northwards. I'll just have a nice hot cup of tea instead (Yorkshire Extra Strong!).

Anyway, I don't really do much religion, I've supported Birmingham City so long that I became an atheist many years ago after countless prayers were never answered. I suppose the Brummies' are like the Egyptians – Moses is on the other side.

Talking of Football News – Stop Press!!! Birmingham City relegation woes are tempered by the Europa League fixtures being announced this morning.

Here are the first 3 rounds of fixtures:

Round 1: Rapid Decline Round 2: Rapid Exit Round 3: Inter Administration

Keep Right On …

M

My reply *– I don't do religion either MP, that's why JS in particular likes to try and make me see the light.*

Chapter 13
Day 7 – I Love It When a Plan Comes Together!

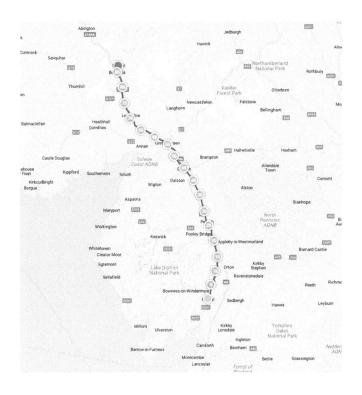

I loved the A team…proper Saturday teatime escapism!

Anyway, using Hannibal as my mentor, today was all about planning…I'd seen the weather forecast and there was a large dollop of very wet rain blowing up from the south. I was due to get to Moffat (about 10 miles north of Lockerbie) today and the rain was due there "early evening".

Only one thing for it then, dawn was 4.30 am so I set the alarm for 4 am and was out of the hotel at 5…with a bit of luck, I'd be safely ensconced in my hotel in Moffat before it rained.

However, such planning didn't go without challenges, especially for the first three hours…first off it was cold…very cold…I'd set off with shorts, under armour and two T-shirts but to be honest, the tights were going to have to come out…sort of cycling shorts but full length down to the ankles…they were my last purchase before I packed and on trying them on my delightful 12-year-old son gave his considered opinion – "You can't wear them, Dad, you look right stupid." (My son can be a bit forthright and to the point at times – I've no idea where he gets that from!)

So, with Ben's words still ringing in my ears, I was really loath to put them on…but it was cold and the last thing I needed was a pulled calf, so on they went, along with the (not very) waterproof top and it was a case of substance over style!

The second problem was Shap Fell, a three-mile long grade 3 hill, straight after a one-mile grade 5 hill…but with no one else about, the hill was conquered and at the top I was looking down on some clouds!

Descending down the other side was more fun but by the time I'd stopped for a spot of breakfast, I'd done 18 miles in three hours.

I pushed on a bit to Carlisle which is about 45 miles from the start and then made a very good decision. I wasn't happy that the tyres were pumped up enough. The tyre wall says 55–80 psi...well the small hand pump can't get any more air in once it's at 55 anyway, plus taking the pump off the valve always releases some air. Anyway, there's a Halfords on the way in to Carlisle and after five minutes of me hinting about wanting to pump my tyres up but hand pumps not being up for the job but a track pump being too big to buy and carry, the assistant finally twigged and invited me to bring the bike in and they'd use their track pump. It turns out that the back tyre was at 50psi, so we upped it to 80...! Two stone of bag plus me on it needs every ounce of air it can get.

This made a massive difference and I felt 10 times faster...in fact in the afternoon, I did the whole Carlisle to Moffat section, 45 miles or so, in one go, no stops, and got to the hotel at 5.05 pm...at 5.10 pm it started raining...Ian 1–0 Rain...although I figure it will equalise in the next five days!

I've also had a bit of interaction with other cyclists today. First of all a chap found me just outside Carlisle with maps and apps trying to figure out why I wasn't where I should be (because a farmer didn't like traffic taking shortcuts past his cows and had put a gate in and made a left turn look like the natural run of the road!)...he asked me where I was heading and when I said Gretna, he said, "Well I'm just out for a ride to get some peace, so I'll go to Gretna with you as well...just follow me..." He had a typical Cumbrian accent and full cycling gear on with the exception of a woolly hat instead of his helmet – think Benny from Crossroads and you'll have a good idea of the look.

Then a bit further on, a bloke from Manchester caught up with me and rode with me for about half an hour…this nutter is riding from Manchester to John O'Groats…and then to Lands End…and then home…mind you, he had been training on the cat and fiddle doing about 200 miles a week…I'm not sure he believed me that I'd not done 200 miles in the last year before this trip!

That road from Carlisle to Gretna is fantastic to ride, it hugs the M6 nearly all the way and at one point I was speeding along thinking I might even be able to have a ride with Victoria Pendleton one day (*no, stop it, Ian, it's Sunday and you promised Julie and Susan you'd be deep and meaningful on a Sunday).

Tonight's cold bath was very very cold and the bath was very deep, but I'm showered and feeling very fresh…I hope this means I'm getting fitter and it's not the calm before the storm. I'll have a spot of tea and get off to bed in a bit (remember I've been up since 4).

One thing I nearly forgot…when I did get to Gretna and crossed the border, I did feel a bit emotional. I'd just ridden my bike the full length of England…I might need a tissue when I get to John O'Groats…it could be like watching Free Willy all over again!

That's England done

AL – It actually sounds like you're liking this now!

JA – So you have had interaction with 'other cyclists'?
Does this mean that you have changed over the last week and now consider yourself to be a cyclist?

My Reply – No.

DS – *Hi Ian, I've been following your progress with interest. Sounds like it's getting easier. I've heard of marathon runners hitting "the wall" after 20 miles, but never a Lands End to John O'Groats cyclist hitting it in Cornwall! Probably best to get it out the way early though!*

Anyway, glad to hear you're making good progress. Good luck for "the last hilly bit" or, as it's sometimes called ... Scotland.

STw – *Just got back from holiday and caught up with the Blog. As you know I've been training for my own cycle trip. This is the first time I've done any distance cycling so understand some of the problems/pain you have endured. I have to say, I'm staggered/impressed/blown away with how well you're doing. Think you're over the boarder now so nearly there. Just keep turning the pedals!*

My reply – *Hi STw...just found out from PW that you do yours on Thursday so good luck with that...pray for the wind in your favour....it makes a massive difference...other than that, given that you've done stacks more training than me, it will be a breeze for you.*

Make sure you are out next time we are and we can compare notes over a pint.

Chapter 14
Pure Football Stuff

When you've got this much time on your hands and what you are doing (pointing a bike forwards and pedalling!) is fairly straightforward, then your mind starts to wander. There's normally two directions a bloke's mind goes in that case and you'll be glad to know that this chapter goes in the direction of football and in particular a subject guaranteed to cause disagreement all around... "all-time best football teams". I like to narrow these down a bit so have applied the following criteria to selection:

The first rule is an absolute – you can't choose anyone who has played for your own team...so that rules out Darius Henderson for any Sheffield United fans such as B.

For this exercise, the next rule is that you must have seen them play live...so for me the likes of Kaka and Messi don't qualify but if you don't watch that much live football, then you can waive that rule if you want, but try and make it players who have played in England.

Here's mine that would take some beating:

Gk – Southall (Everton)

Def – Paulo Maldini (AC Milan)
Def – Stuart Pearce (Forest)
Def – Kevin Radcliffe (Everton)

Rw – David White (Man City)
Cm – Glenn Hoddle (Spurs)
Cm – Bryan Robson (Man United)
Lw – Karel Poborsky (Man United)

Fwd – Michael Owen (Liverpool)
Fwd – Jurgen Klinsmann (Spurs)
Fwd – Gianfranco Zola (Chelsea)

AB – Boring!

SJ – not many Wednesday players in there! Can we have a girlie subject tomorrow please I'm not big on football as you know xx

B – Come on SJ read the small print, 2 of the rules exclude Wednesday players and I think we had quite a few girlie subjects, the first line of the poetry is usually female, we've had the Rachel Stevens v quiz and most of the poems are about Bristols and nipples! In fact, the more I think about it there's been a girlie slant all week, not one mention of cars, drills or barbecues!

My Reply – and you say it's me that doesn't listen!

CH – Two left backs out of three defenders? David White? Karel Poborsky?

My Reply – Maldini can play in the middle…David White is the nearest I've seen to Hirsty… Uwe Rossler nearly got in as well for the same reason and Poborsky got in based on the Italy v Czech Republic match I saw at Anfield in Euro 96

CH – On account of you ruling out Di Canio, mine (done in 2 mins flat and somewhat ignoring the played in England rule) would be…

GK Valdes

RB G Neville
CB Hansen
CB Adams
LB

RM
CM Iniesta
CM Hoddle
LM Giggs

F Cantona
F Dalglish

PW – Now you knew I would bite at this, Ian!

First of all, the rules. You must have seen them play live. Completely agree with this, but are you basing your team on what you saw when they played or the fact that you saw them, but then based the decision on what they were like as a player in their career? Example 1 – David White – I completely forgot he existed! – you must have seen him when he ran Wednesday ragged and scored 4 goals. Example 2 – the only time I saw Gazza, he played for Middlesbrough at the latter end of his career and they got stuffed 5–0 – he was a non-entity. I have based my team on the fact that I saw them play, but they might not have been at the best that day.

Secondly, I've applied "the played in England" rule, as you have – i.e., Maldini played in England for Italy/AC Milan, but not for an English team!

Thirdly, excluding the team you support depends on who you support. It probably made no difference to your team (don't tell me you'd have included someone like Hirsty, who played for England once, or Di Canio, who couldn't even get in the Italian team!). It makes a massive difference to mine – World Cup winners and the like!

Another thing, your team has 3 players included that you only saw in that great match at Anfield in Euro 96 (how can I forget our debate about Zola being the best player in the world when he only came on for the last 20 minutes of that match!).

So, this is mine (as a Chesterfield fan!):

Seaman
Cannavaro
Maldini

Adams (Captain)

Cole (though it pains me to say it!)

Vieira

Xavi

Iniesta

Messi

Henry

Bergkamp

If you say I can't include any Arsenal players, then it would be:

Schmeichel

G Neville (again, it pains me to say it, but I found full-backs the hardest to pick)

Cannavaro

Nesta

Maldini

R Keane (Captain)

Xavi

Iniesta

Messi

Ronaldo

Zola

Players I also considered were:

Alan Hanson

Rooney

Rivaldo

Ronaldinho

Shevchenko (of Dynamo Kiev and AC Milan – I never saw him play for Chelsea!)

Dalglish

Gascoigne

Luis Figo

Shearer (my personal memory of him playing was his constant moaning to referees)

Le Tissier

My Reply – *Interesting choices there PW with a few comments that need biting at.*

First of all, David Hirst was better than Shearer and would have had many caps and goals had those 2 thugs Bould and Adams not decided that the only way they could stop him was to injure him.... permanently (although I think it was Arsenal that he still scored against after Bould had broken his ankle!)

Secondly are you trying to tell me that Chris Waddle wouldn't have a chance of getting in if I could choose Wednesday players?

And finally, if you are struggling for a full back may I suggest the best right back ever to play in this country (that's a fact by the way, not subjective)...Roland Nilsson...surely not even your anti Wednesday bias would stop you picking him now I've reminded you?

P.S Hirsty played twice for England not once.

AL – *Had a few problems with the Blackberry so bit late with the team. So many of my favourite players have either played for Wednesday or I've only ever seen on the tele so this was more difficult than I thought it would be. My team is therefore:*

GK Pat Jennings
RB Gary Neville
CB Roger Johnson
CB Tony Adams
LB Stuart Pearce
RM David Beckham
CM Glenn Hoddle
CM Paul Gascoigne
LM Eddie Gray

Up front Michael Owen and Alan Clarke
Sub (as us old uns can remember a time when you could only name one) Kevin Keegan.

I've lost a lot of time thinking about this. Please don't set a similar challenge I've got to get stuff done!

MP – *Here is my team. As per your rules – as personally seen and not Birmingham City. From Sept 70 onwards:*

Goalkeeper – Gordon Banks (Stoke City)
Def – Bobby Moore (West Ham and Fulham)
Def – Norman Hunter (Leeds)
Def – Paul Reaney (Leeds)
Def – Paul McGrath (Aston Villa)
Mid – David Beckham (Man Utd)
Mid – Paul Scholes (Man Utd)
Mid – Billy Bremner (Leeds)
Striker – Kenny Dalglish (Liverpool)

Striker – Bobby Charlton (Man Utd)

Striker – George Best (Man Utd & Fulham)

Best Birmingham Players – Joe Hart, Frank Worthington, Trevor Francis, Bob Hatton, Christophe Dugarry.

Bonny Scotland awaits!

K.R.O.

My Reply – *No Bob Latchford in your list of Birmingham players…? And didn't he have a brother who played in the net for you…? And where's Graham Hyde?*

Glenn Hoddle, one of the most popular choices

Chapter 15
Day 8 – What a Fantastic, Brilliant Day

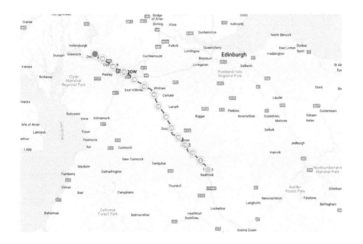

Up until now, when people have asked me if I'm enjoying myself, the answer has been that I've had more of a sense of achievement than enjoyment, but today I've really enjoyed myself for a variety of reasons.

First off the pain in my backside is close to 1/10 and even my gentleman's equipment is in fine fettle…! Slight numbness in bits of hands and fingers but no pain anymore… physically I'm a fine specimen (OK that might be pushing it a bit but not much hurts).

Today started with a reminder that the Scots don't do "early". Whenever I play golf up here, we always struggle to get early breakfast and on asking in the hotel last night if I could get an early breakfast, I got a very friendly "oh aye, the chef will be here at 8 so you can have breakfast soon after that…" 8 o'clock has never been early, I meant 6 but given that the run from Moffat to Dumbarton was only (relatively) 70 miles, I decided to have a lie in and leave at 9.

Which I did…straight out of Moffat and uphill…and up…and up…and up…above the clouds…! And I got caught by a guy from Leicester who is also doing LEJOG and who hates Leicester because he loves sea fishing and there isn't a sea in Leicester! I wonder how long he lived there before he found that out…! Anyway, from above the clouds there was then the way down to a normal altitude…which was fun.

I rode with this guy for a bit and then I stopped for a break and he carried on…then I got caught by the nutter from yesterday who is cycling to John O'Groats first before then going down to Lands End and then cycling home. I wonder what are the odds on him catching a train at some point? I had a chat with him for about half an hour and then he had a stop off but not before warning me about the forthcoming hill!

Now one other thing I might not have mentioned is that the main reason I'm doing LEJOG and not JOGLE is that the prevailing winds in the UK are supposed to be from the South West…and wind in your face is a cyclist's worst enemy…well the winds were from the south west today, but mainly from the west…and while LEJOG is predominantly travelling north and east, today's route was 80% to the west…straight in to a very strong wind…at times it was like pedalling in treacle, especially on the flat when it felt like uphill still.

But because I felt so fit and well today, I saw it as a challenge. At times I was laughing at the absurdity of what I was trying to do…uphill…into the wind…I must be mad…but I was loving it. I'd done about 45 miles before I stopped for lunch in Hamilton and quickly found out that I'd forgotten one major thing I should have brought with me. An interpreter. The conversation went like this…

Me: "Can I have the vegetable soup and a ham toastie please?"

Girl behind counter: "Do you want that to eat in or take away?" (Well that's what I eventually worked out was what she'd said.)

Me…stares blankly trying to work out what she could possibly have said that can be remotely connected to my order: "Diet coke, please!"

And I'm only at Glasgow…experience tells me the further north I go, the stronger the accent! Anyway, refreshed, I push on through Glasgow…at about 5 o'clock…good planning, Ian!

But it wasn't too bad actually and the main challenge was avoiding pedestrians rather than cars.

I then had an amusing moment at some traffic lights. I'm sitting there waiting for them to go green and a Chav in his souped up Saxa or the like pulls up at the side of me…music as loud as he could, windows open and he looks over at me, no doubt expecting a shake of the head or some middle-aged rant about the music being too loud.

What he actually saw was a 45-year-old, slightly rotund bloke, Lycra clad in a fluorescent orange T-shirt who was feeling incredibly happy singing along at the top of his voice to his chavy music…because it turns out that airplanes by B.o.B (feat. Hayley Williams) is one of Ben's favourites and I've had to have it on almost every time he's been in the car for the last six months.

"Can we pretend that airplanes in the night sky are like shooting stars…I could really use a wish right now…wish right now…wish right now."

Lights go green and off he roars as fast as he can.

"Oi, come back here…I was listening to that."

But he was gone…as fast as he could, away from the old Lycra nutter that he'd come across unexpectedly in the middle of Glasgow!

And on I went, through Glasgow and out through Clydebank to my hotel. And it was at this moment that I had very poignant thoughts…because the road out alongside the river Clyde reminded me so much of the road out of the centre of Sheffield to the east…the large swathes of derelict land where the shipyards used to be and the boarded up premises where supporting small businesses were and the pubs, no longer with any thirsty workmen to make them a viable proposition could easily have been the same roads along Attercliffe in Sheffield. The only difference being the shipyards would have been steelworks. Interestingly enough, barber shops were still going…as they are in the equivalent areas of Sheffield. I suppose you always need your hair cut whatever you are doing in life!

Now I don't very often sit on the fence regarding many things in life but my feelings over how we've allowed the industries such as coal mining, steelmaking and shipbuilding to become almost non-existent in this country are very mixed. On the one hand we need to move on...there's nothing clever about having to go a mile or more underground to find materials to burn to provide energy and if other countries can do it cheaper, then we should channel our energies in to new, alternative industries. But the fact that we've put whole generations and communities out to grass...workers who would regularly shed blood, sweat and tears for their employers, is a travesty...we really should have built for the future before we shut down the present...both my grandparents and parents worked in such industries and it's all part of me being what I am today...but I wouldn't for one minute want to do that type of job or wish it for my son, hence my mixed feelings.

Anyway, enough moping about the past...I'm in a brand-new Premier Inn just south of Loch Lomond and am really looking forward to tomorrow...30 miles of flat along the banks of the Loch to start...about 20 miles of flat in to Fort William and the base of Ben Nevis to finish...in between...40 miles of hills...some steep, some long...but apparently there's a ten-mile downhill stretch in to Glen Coe towards the end so that should be something to savour. The weather looks set fair for tomorrow, if not for after that!

Hope everyone is well and please share a thought for my father-in-law who ended up in A&E this afternoon after a nasty fall outside his home...hope you are feeling better soon. (Sharon, you'll have to pass that on as I don't for one minute think your dad will have picked up the laptop and decided to read my blog!!!)

As a special request (see comments below), we also have another dilemma question today.

Zara Phillips or Jessica Ennis?

JS – Oh Ian, If I was choosing, I would have Jessica most defo.

SM – Well I'm pleased you had a great day – the equivalent of a runners high hit you today and it sounds fab! Now what really is heartening is your deep and meaningful thoughts. Sounds like they took you by surprise, they were much better for me than yesterdays. They were very personal to you – that's good and they made you think about the world you live in & who you are and what made you this way. I couldn't ask for more. You've always been good at writing but maybe you need to do more of this reflective stuff. I enjoyed it. S x

B – All this deep-thinking lark really does take all my time and energy and whilst we are on the subject of deep thoughts can you do the 'today's dilemma' a bit earlier in the day, just like a black coffee it stimulates my mind and sets me up for the day!

PW – You seem to be enjoying it more and more, Ian – you're proving all of us wrong and I'm sure that's a big motivation to you. Hope you're having a great day (weather's great down here, so hope you're getting the same). You've got some avid followers in our office – e.g., the boys doing the Coast to Coast at the end of the week……seems like you've stole their thunder a bit…. Mr Tw's got no excuses now! Speak soon.

AL – *Jess…not even a contest this one. She the fittest bird in Sheff by miles! Keep pedalling dude*

My reply – *That's as may be but seeing as I'm covering the country scouring for decent women (although Sharon thinks it's for charity) I can cast my net a bit wider than Sheffield!*

SJ – *Thank you Ian for thinking of my dad. He's had a night at our house and returned home now (just in case you were thinking you would have to make your trip last longer!) He tells me he's fine, but his face and eyes say otherwise but what can I do bless him. I'm so glad you had a good day, you sounded so happy and upbeat when we spoke last night, I hope today wasn't too hard and that you managed to tackle the hills with vim & vigour. Speak soon xxx*

B – *Jessica, fantastic stomach and more likely to bump into her at the sandwich shop on Neepsend! Full Stop Cafe also used by Arctic Monkeys and me!*

PB – *Zara, all day. She's all woman and marrying an egg chaser! Jess, although cute is far too tiny!*

MC – *Jess would be the girlfriend and Zara for the weekend when Jess is competing. (always keep your options open)*

PM – *Got to be Jess. Can't believe anyone would use their posh totty allowance up on Zara when Pippa is available!*

AB – *Who is Jessica Ennis? I'm confused now!*

AB – *Any chance you could post a dilemma for us girls?*

My Reply – *No*

B – *To make these ramblings more appealing to both sexes, can I suggest you throw in a dilemma for the ladies, Cillit Bang or Jif? Sorry for the young and trendy that's Cif.*

Chapter 16
Let's Have a Rant and
Let It All Out

Every now and then it's good to just let it all out at things in life that get on your nerves.

Not the major stuff that we all get annoyed with but what many would see as minor at best (or worst depending on which way you look at it). In some cases others will see things as good but you want to have a proper blow out at…such as these!

Vending machine operators…don't put Kit Kats on the top shelf…when they drop all that way and hit the bottom, they break in to loads of pieces…I want my Kit Kat in four sticks not 57 bits (and while I'm on the subject, a two-stick Kit Kat should be labelled "half a Kit Kat")…same goes for cans of pop, guess what happens when you open one of those after it's dropped eight feet to be served!

Apple…now I'm not about to tell you how to run your company, clearly you are doing something right, but you need to sort your shops out…it's all well and good having loads of spotty geeks milling around with their blue T-shirts, fancy gadgets and being so excited when you ask them to show you how something works, but at some point you need to be able to pay for something…and for that we need a till. I've flounced out of two shops last month after being told to "find someone with a blue T-shirt and they'll take your money…" only to walk from one side of the shop to the other and back again being avoided by geeks because they can see I want to pay, which is akin to some kind of work and they'd much rather talk to some other kids about gizmos.

Hotel bed maker uppers…stop tucking the bloody quilt (that's a duvet for any posh people) in at the bottom…what's that all about…? I want my feet stuck out of the bed when I'm asleep, not feeling like I'm in a straitjacket…and what's that silly strip of material across the bottom all about as well…just something else to be moved.

Energy saving light bulb manufacturers…how about you start making them emit some light or just call them "bulbs".

The Chase. Brilliant quiz programme hosted by Bradley Walsh for an hour each teatime, but for God's sake, you could cut it down to 20 minutes if you didn't ask the other three contestants, every single time, what the player should go for. "You've got £5,000, low offer is £1,000, high offer is £26,000, what do you think they should do?"

Almost without fail each person for every contestant in every one of the 17,000 episodes that they've recorded says, "Low offer is an insult, you are much better than that…£26,000 is tempting but stay safe and get back to us with £5,000…" and that is what they do (stay safe, not always get back).

And then there's the stupid comment that the chaser and Walsh come out with when it's all over and the three players in the final have lost:

"Unlucky, you needed Neil in the final with you, he'd have made all the difference, he was a good player" – really? If he was that good, then how come three got through and he was the only one who got knocked out?

And the coup de grace of it all is when three players have built a nice prize fund between them of around £20,000 and the last player:

"I'll go for the low offer of minus £3,000 please…I fancy a slice of their money without having to risk much…I know I'm really stealing £1000 off each of them but who cares, it's all about me."

The programme would be better if they put a baseball bat with each of the contestants for when that final player "comes back".

Old people…you are retired, you've got all day to do stuff, so please do it while younger people are at work…don't go swimming between 6 and 9 in the morning and then treat it like a wet coffee morning while others are trying to swim around you…do that about 11 am, then you can have some lunch and nip to the bank about 3 pm.

Banks…now it's not very often I come in to a branch and I know that's how you like it, but occasionally, just occasionally, I have a need to use your counter service…50p in the pay and display for 30 minutes, five-minute walk to the bank, five minutes in there and five minutes back…15 minutes to spare…so the last thing I really need is to see a snaking queue (of old people!) and then to hear you having a chat with each and every one of them when they've done what they want to do. No, they don't want an ISA, money is for under the mattress, no they don't want to change their insurance policy, they've been paying 50p a week to that nice young man from the Pru for about 60 years now and they aren't about to change just because they can save £800 a year... Just serve them, smile nicely and move on to the next person...please!

This drives me nuts...always has...just put it back the right way...typical of the slack, oh it will do attitude that too many people have!!!

Airlines...when you serve me a meal (if you can call it that!) with a nice soft roll and a small packet of butter...that has been stored at sub-zero temperatures…do you really think a brittle plastic knife is going to make any impact on spreading it?

And some quick-fire ones that need no explanation:

People stopping at the top of an escalator to decide which way to go.

Uber (and Uber eats) drivers.

Fishing.

Hay Fever.

Airline passengers trying to get a case with three weeks' worth of luggage into the overhead locker.

People not in BMWs using the outside lane of the motorway.

Highways agency taking six weeks to do some road works and then six months block paving a few bits to make it look pretty…whilst we all tootle past at 10mph.

Jazz music.

Supermarkets that don't have aisles that go straight up and down – you know who you are!

That moment in life where your child stops leaving half their meal for you to finish.

People.

Brown nosers at work.

Real Ale.

Postie's leaving elastic bands all over the place.

Wind chimes.

Opera.

Ballet.

Walking dead.

People who don't thank you when you've let them out at a junction in your car Other than that, I think I'm a pretty laid-back person!

JA – Ahh – the real Ian is back!
Tucked in bedding drives me mad too.

AL – Didn't take long really did it!

B – Bye bye Bill Oddie, welcome back Jeremy Clarkson.
There used to be a grate cover like that in the middle of the road on the Sheffield side of the A57 at Ladybower. Annoyed me so much I considered setting up my own traffic management system to correct it. Nothing other than slack or done intentionally to annoy everyone!

My reply – if you do then can you use those manual stop/go boards and can I have one end.... I've always fancied that job; I'll even start smoking so I can have the obligatory fag hanging out of one corner of my mouth and anyone who even thinks about looking at me the wrong way is in for a long wait irrespective of if anything is coming the other way.

Chapter 17
Day 9 – Mixed Feelings

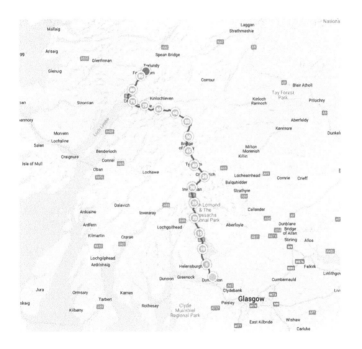

It's starting to worry me…every day I have mixed feelings…at this rate I could start to develop grey areas in my life and that would be a disaster!

At around 5 o'clock I rode in to Fort William like Woody on Bullseye…shorts and T-shirt, sun on my back, wind in the right direction and 90 miles over some serious hills all behind me…how good a day had that been?

Well, if I'm honest, mixed…! and not as good as I'd expected…perhaps I'd expected too much and thought every day was going to get better, especially the Loch Lomond to Ben Nevis leg. It all started OK, up at 4 am, out by 5 (complete with packing up for breakfast as there was no chance of an early one in the hotel) and a ride along the banks of Loch Lomond. What a disappointment it was, on two major levels. Firstly it was cold again at that time and secondly the road along the side of Loch Lomond could have been a road almost anywhere…because all you can see is trees! Sights of the Loch are few and far between despite it being only a few feet away.

But I made good time and at about 7 am I came to a picnic area by the Loch which seemed a good place to stop and have breakfast. Half an hour later and I'm off again eventually coming to Crianlarich where I decided to have something substantial to eat at the tea bar on the station. This proved to be a very good idea because the next time I saw anywhere that served food or drink was nearly 40 miles later in Glen Coe.

And leaving the tea bar at Crianlarich is where it all started to go wrong. The climb up the hill to the plains above Glen Coe was challenging but well worth the views and stunning scenery once you are up there and the payback comes in the promise of a 10 mile slightly downhill stretch. What I wasn't prepared for was the howling gale that was blowing straight up Glen Coe…straight into my face…working hard to get up hills is challenging, expected and rewarding when you get there, but having to work nearly as hard on the flat and downhill is just very very frustrating and by the time I stopped for a bite to eat in Glen Coe, I was totally fed up. If there had been a railway station with a train on the platform going south, then I would have got on it there and then. I spent an hour there and cheered myself up with the knowledge that in five miles I turned about 180 degrees and the wind would be at my back.

And it was, which was how I ended up breezing into Fort William in such a good mood.

So that's day 9… Just about 200 miles to go now and it's done…Physically I am still sort of OK, although I've over extended my right knee a couple of times today trying to push hard when in too low a gear so I need to be careful of that and I think I've damaged nerves in both my hands, hopefully not permanently!

And I'd like to finish on what I consider to be a specialist subject of mine. Toilet roll holder positioning…ideally, they should be on a wall, within arm's reach of the toilet…not too close, not too far away and definitely not, the Ben Nevis Hotel in Fort William, on the bloody wall directly behind you!!!

Oh, and one more thing…I've forgotten to mention on previous posts, one of the great things about this trip has not only been the challenge and the sights I've seen, but more than anything, the main difference between travelling by car and by bike is what you hear…I'm amazed how noisy the birds are and how many of them are chirping away at any one time. You can hear the rabbits scuttling away on the road edge verges when you approach (and there are thousands of them!), you can hear water lapping at the edges of lochs and streams and waterfalls running where you would never know they existed.

Loch Lomond at 7 am

CH – *Did I just read that right?*
You sound like a changed man, who now prefers his bike, tweeting birds and the great outdoors to flashing people till they get out of the fast lane.

What next? Vegetarian?

Oh, and one thing I keep forgetting to ask you. When you are on your bike, and all is going well, do you sing? I do. I can't help it. Especially if I'm on my own, with not many people around me, and especially in the countryside.

Or is it just me?

SJ *– Ian you definitely do sound like a changed man, who would have ever thought you would have grey areas in your life…. long may this continue. Maybe you should do this more often. I'm so looking forward to meeting the 'new Ian' xxx*

DS *– What species of birds? Looking forward to chatting this thru' with you!*

Keep going mate.

PM – *Where's the real Ian? Getting back to nature & I think you even mentioned eating vegetables at one point. What sort of example does that set Ben? I'm sure once you get back behind the wheel of the gas guzzler with a McDonalds meal in hand you'll return to normal. Great achievement so far.*

JS *– Ian, you sound like a changed man! well done you are a star!*

JA – *Shall we run a sweep on how long it takes until the 'real Ian' returns?*

My pound is that it is before he gets to Edinburgh on the return journey – as someone on the train will have annoyed him by then.

Well done Ian – a great achievement! Sharon & I will toast your success in the pub on Friday night.

__SJ__ – I Think you are right on that one – he'll have wrapped his bike around someone's neck way before getting to Chesterfield! That's a great idea Jo we'll raise a glass to celebrate his achievement…be rude not to! See you Friday.

__AL__ – You sound in better nick than I thought you would be at this stage bloke. Every now and then I wish I'd said I'd do it and quickly reality sets in and I'm glad I'm sat in McDonalds with my healthy tea! Keep going dude 200miles more seems like a doddle now.

Out of interest how and when are you getting home?

__My Reply__ – First off I need to get from JoG to Thurso when I've done on Friday which is about 20 miles…. I could cycle but I think the odds are more and more becoming in favour of a taxi!

On Satdi I catch the 0647 from Thurso to Inverness then Inverness to Edinburgh then Edinburgh to Chesi…Then I will cycle the 2 minutes down the hill from the station to home…. get in about 8 pm I think.

__AL__ – I won't offer to pick you up then! Have a massive bacon sarni and a cheeky beer on the train back bloke. I don't believe all this changed man b****x!

My Reply – I'm Glad you don't believe it because it's not true!

MP – Ian, you're doing great Buddy. As we say at St Andrews:
Keep right on to the end of the Road...
(Harry Lauder – Scotland)
Cheers
KRO
M
PS If u bump into Alex McLeish – give him a dig for me.

RM – Good luck with the ride mate – really impressed!

AM – Hi Ian, I have just caught up again with all your blog – you're doing brilliant, I bet Ben is so proud of his dad despite looking "reight stupid" in the tights! Love the photos!

Chapter 18
Day 10 – Struggling for Words

I suppose today was everything I thought yesterday would be, I can't think of any negatives about it and hopefully I can get over to everyone, what a brilliant day this has been. As I'd gotten a relatively short trip of 65 miles planned, I had a bit of a lie in and breakfast in the hotel for a change which included one of my favourites, haggis.

Looking at the three different websites for a weather forecast, I came to the conclusion that they really didn't have a clue, or to use weather jargon, there were going to be "localised showers" so I set off when I was ready at about 8.30 am.

I rode out of town in the shadow of Ben Nevis (well there would have been a shadow had there been any sun!) and made good progress for around eight miles to Spean Bridge where high on the hill there is a memorial to the commandos who apparently have done a lot of training there in the past. I must admit I shed a tear or two here. It's one thing reading tributes to 79-year-old WW2 veterans, it's another reading of 22-year-olds killed in not only wars many years ago but in more recent times in conflicts such as the Falklands, Afghanistan and Iraq.

This was another brilliant example of why I decided to do the ride. I had no idea this place existed and even an hour or so earlier it wasn't something I expected to come across and yet here I was, with tears in my eyes, marvelling at the monument and the views and reading with utmost respect the tributes to those who had paid the ultimate sacrifice to allow us to lead the relatively free lives that we do.

Once I had composed myself, I rode on from Spean Bridge and past Loch Lochy…which was everything I expected Loch Lomond to be yesterday. Absolutely stunning views with the water lapping gently at the road side and no trees in the way to spoil the view – brilliant. And then, remembering how I enjoyed a time "off road" on the canal path around Morecambe Bay, I diverted on to the

Caledonian Canal tow path for about five miles to Fort Augustus where there is a lock complex. Again, what a brilliant site. I can't believe I have stumbled across this place so soon after Spean Bridge. I feel like someone has decided it's treat day today and has spent the night dropping these places on my route. I spent ten minutes or so just sitting, gaping at the locks in action like I was an eight-year-old all over again. It's a bit like watching planes take off and land, no matter how old you are you still have to watch and marvel at it.

One of the many locks at Fort Augustus

I am fascinated by how simple they are compared to what they achieve...allowing boats to move up and down hills...who would even think about doing something like that? Leonardo Da Vinci is apparently the answer to that question. For a bloke best known for painting pictures I can't believe how under publicised his involvement in the inventions of canal locks and helicopters is.

And then I have to leave what feels like my own personal sweet shop which is bathed in glorious warm sunshine and continue north eastward up to Loch Ness which needs no introduction. The A9 follows the Loch from start to finish, although it is a bit hilly in places there are some great views.

There was a spot of light rain on my way up the side of Loch Ness but such was my mood that we'll call it a cool down. I had a spot of lunch at a pub at Invermoriston which is about a quarter of the way up the Loch and then a drink just over an hour later at the delightfully named Drumnadrochit before ploughing on to the end of Loch Ness and picking up again on the Caledonian Canal and River Ness into Inverness and the comfort of my hotel.

Even the last few miles to the hotel were amusing.

In a nutshell, I couldn't find it! I know I should have prepared more and that day one lycra geek will have printouts of where he is staying but I asked for directions from seven different people and only one got me anywhere near where I wanted to be…I even rang the hotel and the very friendly chap on reception there told me:

"Can you see the police headquarters?"

"Yes, I'm right outside it now."

"OK, go down the road at the side of it."

"Which road, the one to the left or to the right?"

"Ooh, that's a good question."

Yes, I know it is but a fairly reasonable one, don't you think?

So he goes on. "Well, if you see Tesco's then turn left there."

Now Tesco's was opposite the police HQ so I figured it must be the road between the two...40 minutes later on arriving at the hotel and seeing another Tesco just around the corner I work out that he didn't mean the Tesco that he must have known I could see...but he gave me a nice smile and said, "Ah well, it's a nice evening for a bike ride."

Indeed it was sir, but not necessarily what you want if you've just done 70 miles...! But I'd had a great day and so I smiled nicely back at him and went for a cold bath and a well-earned spot of food.

One thing I did notice today is that all the rivers and Lochs have crystal clear waters and at the edge so did the Caledonian Canal. But apart from a foot or so in the edge, the canal itself was jet black. I've no idea why and even a quick google didn't seem to help out. I can only think it must be really, really deep.

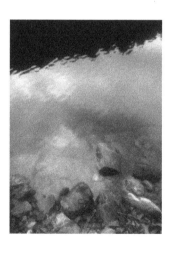

The dark waters of the Caledonian Canal

So, what a brilliant day…I even had an involuntary quick tour of Inverness at the end to look around and burn off a bit of excess energy and can't wait for tomorrow.

Which is when I will be in the middle of nowhere…ending up in a farmhouse near a place called Dunbeath…will they have Wi-Fi? I'd be surprised…will orange have coverage…I'd be amazed…so the next time I update everyone on progress may well be from John O'Groats or Thurso on Friday when I've finished (God willing)…or even Edinburgh on the way home on Saturday. So if I don't get chance, I'd like to thank everyone now for all their support and kind donations and for engaging with me on what would otherwise have been a very lonely journey.

This was the day that had made everything worthwhile. Thanks everyone. Take care.

Injury news

So there I was taking a photo of Nessie and I decided to lean over the fence as I didn't want it to spoil the photo. As I moved back over the fence, I caught my arm on the top of it…severe barbed wire fence top!

It caused a deep cut, nay gash, in my arm near the elbow and ripped a gaping wound a bit further down my arm.

First diagnosis was it needs about 15–20 stitches…possibly more…should I call for a paramedic or pedal on to Inverness where I could get it done at A&E? But wait…I've got a mini first aid kit in the bag and inspired by Mick Lyons having his wound stitched at the side of the pitch during the Wednesday v Liverpool League Cup quarter final in 1983, I decided to stitch it myself at the roadside...plasters, antiseptic wipes, swabs, gauze, scissors...but no needle...or thread...what kind of first aid kit is this?

By the time I'd taken the first aid kit apart, I had managed to stem the bleeding and so decided to press on and get it sorted in Inverness.

But guess what...by the time I got there, I'd forgotten about it and one shower later it was healed and almost disappeared...all that talk of Jesus and Moses earlier in the trip must have rubbed off and a wound needing over 30 stitches was gone...fantastic!

Seeing as I injured myself taking the photo, then the least I can do is show you the resulting effort...and my injury

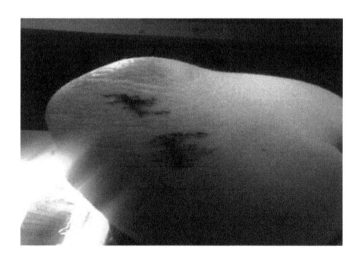

The gaping wound requiring 30 stitches

The resulting photo

And today's dilemma...Pippa Middleton or Tina off Corrie?

LJ – *Looks Lovely, you have almost inspired me to have a go myself; but I did say almost!*

AL – *Tough one. Tina off corrie wins as Pippa may be a bit posh for me.*

SJ – *Pippa definitely. I'm starting to think that you may be spending far too much time on your own as all you're thinking about is women lol and your blogs are getting much shorter. Its OK for you, you've only got to do the ride and then write about it. We, on the other hand, have to sit here waiting to hear what exciting titbits you have to offer us each day. You don't realise how hard that is so please stop being selfish and get back to writing again. Thank you Love you xxx*

CH – *As I'm too busy and aloof to bother watching soaps, I'd go for Pippa. What's wrong with posh? She is fit and loaded to boot.*

PM – *I don't know who Tina is but even if I did she'd have to be fit to beat Pippa. I agree with the previous reply nothing wrong with a bit of posh for a change. Hope our lass doesn't see this!*

SJ – *Ouch!*

AL – *I was discussing that game with Pete McDermott today! How weird is that?*

Chapter 19
Day 11 – I Think I'm Beat

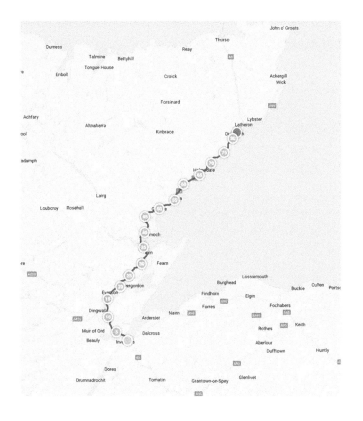

Absolutely knackered. I can't believe how hard today has been. Not mentally because I know how close I am to the finish but physically in three or four different ways, today has been very hard. It's as if someone has thought, "he's starting to find this easy, let's show him how hard it can be".

So for starters, today's route was 85 miles and whilst not the longest day, it wasn't far off. When I got up this morning, I think I'd gone past the "getting fitter" stage and am now starting to feel physically very tired.

Anyway, I set off about 7.15 am and did a good 10 miles out of Inverness before stopping for some breakfast. Then I did about another 15 miles over some really nice bridges over the Inverness, Moray, Cromarty and Dornoch Firth's that reminded me of the shipping forecast on Radio 4 long wave that always interrupted the cricket in the days before I got a car with a fancy DAB radio (oh how I am missing my car).

I stopped again for a break and when I started off again that's when it first went…something muscular in my left thigh. At first I thought I could ride it off, but it wouldn't go away and it was one of those strange ones…it wasn't painful when weight bearing, just when my thigh was at an angle of 45 degrees to my body…which happens to be every turn of the pedal! Initially it didn't make any difference whether I was sitting pedalling or off the saddle but eventually it became so painful that I couldn't stand and again could only use low gears.

I stopped for some lunch around 12 and went in a chemist's next door for some strapping and Ibuleve gel…patched myself up a bit over lunch and started out again. The pain was a bit more bearable but I still couldn't stand and pedal so I was just going to have to take it slow.

It's on the scoreboard now.

I had a break in the afternoon and then stopped for some tea in a place called Helmersdale at 5.30 pm. At 6.30 I started out on the last 15 miles to my hotel...straight up a big hill...to put it in to perspective for those who know it, this hill was a bit like the climb from Glossop, just east of Manchester over the Pennine's on the A57 snake pass to the top before it descends in to the outskirts of Sheffield...about as long and as steep.

Last night in Inverness it went dark about 11 pm. Tonight it went dark at about 6.35 pm. And then it started to spit with rain. I could see what was going to happen here and quickly got all the gear on the back covered up with waterproofs and put my slightly shower proof jacket on…and then it got darker…and the rain got heavier and the hill got steeper…and it kept raining…and I kept going (well what else could I do?) Finally I got to the top and came down the other side…but it was still raining heavily and there was water everywhere so I had to be very careful and had my hands on the brakes nearly all the way down to the bottom…where I encountered.

Another hill…about the same as the first one…imagine cycling to the top of the snake pass and back down only to be told to go back up again…! Everything was wet and heavier and I was cold…my gloves were soaking and cold and I was really worried about being able to pull the brakes on when needed.

And then it just stopped and off it went over the North Sea, leaving some spectacular views behind it of the hills to one side and the North Sea with its oil rigs on the horizon on the other. Scotland really is a beautiful country but can be brutal when it wants to be.

What really touched me at this time was that at least three different lorries coming down the hills I was slowly ascending, took the time to stop, wind down their windows and ask if I was alright and did I need anything or any help. I resisted the temptation to ask them to turn around and give me a lift to Dunbeath but the very fact that they had all done this gave me an extra round of energy.

The ride down the other side of this second hill took me in to Dunbeath which was my bed for the night, in particular about one mile further north at a place called Tormore Farm.

Bearing in mind that most hotels I've stayed in have been Travelodge's or Premier Inn's where all booking is done on line and with credit cards, this booking, over the telephone, went something like this…

Phone rings and is answered…

"Hello!"

"Hi, is that Tormore Farm bed and breakfast?"

"Aye, what do you want?"

"I was wondering if you had any vacancies on 16 June?"

"Aye…OK, we'll see you then."

"Er…do you want my name or anything?"

"Aye, OK what is it?"

"It's Ian Jenkins and do you want my credit card details?"

"Nay, just show up."

And that was it…! And show up I did at about 9 o'clock. It is a working farm with what I consider to be a proper bed and breakfast run by an old lady while her husband and sons do the farming bit. My bike is in the barn with loads of other machinery and I'm in a room with a double bed, old wardrobe and sideboard with loads of glass ornaments that are on ornate cotton doily thingies…and there's no en-suite. The bathroom is just down the hallway and there is no shower, just a bath! (If I was with my wife, we would currently be in the car heading back down the A9 looking for the nearest 4-star hotel!)

So that was day 11 done. Nothing amusing to report today, just a very long hard slog over some challenging terrain with very challenging weather at times and a left thigh that's about had enough. But only 36 miles left and

I'm sure with a good night's sleep it will manage four hours or so cycling in the morning.

What is also very important tomorrow is that the football league fixtures for next season are out... My man didn't let me down today with texting me the League Cup draw so I'm assuming he hasn't done anything daft like booking himself a meeting at 10 in the morning?

SP – Hope Peak FM got in touch. Felt we just wanted to do something. So impressed. And "grey" impresses me as well. You should be so chuffed. Absolutely well done. Looking forward to luring you for a pint on Saturday night.

AL – Today sounds a nightmare bloke but you've nearly done it. Hope the injury doesn't mess up the last day. Well done fella. Don't know if you've seen the cricket score. They ended the day 81–4

And I've got a meeting in Coventry is at 10.30 am so should be able to get the fixtures to you before I go in.

Enjoy the B&B!

SJ – Please please tell me the bed didn't have wool blankets, or worse still, a candlewick bedspread – I'm horrified just reading about it!!!

You have done fantastically well and we're so proud of you. I would have given up at Lands End. Hope tomorrow is a much better day and the thigh injury holds up for you xxx

B – Don't worry I'll let you know when your 2 big games are. UTB FTO

SJ – What does UTB FTO mean? Am I being really thick? I've seen it a few times!

B – Up the Blades, not sure about the other bit, possibly flipping trumpy Owls or maybe something not so complimentary.

SJ – Oh right thank you B. I've also seen something similar that an Owls fan had written so I presume theirs said UTO FTB. Hope SM and the boys are well and hopefully we'll see you for a night out soon so Ian can talk us through his trip – knowing Ian I'm sure lots (& lots) of photos will be involved too xxx

Chapter 20
Day 12 – What Have I Got Left?

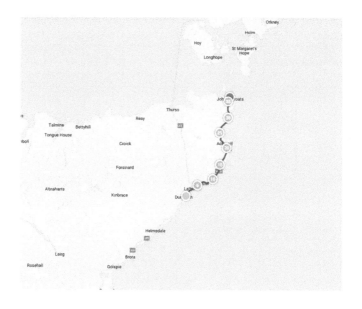

Morning

Only 38 miles or so to go today, so I got up for breakfast around 8 am to see glorious sunshine outside. The homemade farmhouse breakfast wasn't as good as I'd expected but it filled a hole and I got ready to set off in to the sunshine at about 9. And it's a good job it was sunny because if you cast your mind back to last night, I'd arrived wet…very wet!

The host had offered me the use of the towel rail in the bathroom to dry things on, only I'm not sure it was left on all night and come this morning, most things were still damp. This wasn't a problem for a lot of stuff as I'd got spare dry ones but if you remember back even further, you may recall that I'd taken to wearing two pairs of cycling shorts in an attempt to solve the bottom issue…two being every pair I'd got…! and the shoes were still wet…not damp, wet!

But as I say, it's great out so off I set and I have covered 20 miles in to Wick along what is basically a cliff top road with brilliant views over the North Sea. The left thigh is still sore and tender, nowhere near as painful as yesterday but I daren't risk standing on it so I'm going to take my time.

I spent five minutes having a chat to the bloke from Manchester who is cycling to John O'Groats before going to Lands End and then back home. Well, he's been to John O'Groats and is now on his way back down but has decided it's too much like hard work and he's just going straight home to Manchester. That's just shy of 1,000 miles without actually doing LEJOG one way or the other! Mad.

PW – Home straight now – well done, mate. Enjoy the views and completing your once in a lifetime achievement. Speak soon!

JA – Well done Ian. Look forward to the final updates. It will give SJ, ABX & I something to talk about in the pub tonight – cos we often struggle for conversation.

SJ – Good point J, at least we'll have something to talk about rather than the usual standing in the pub looking blankly at each other haha! See you later.

SJ – I've just had a thought...how are we going to manage without your daily blog to entertain us Ian? Maybe you could keep it going just with your everyday trials & tribulations x.

My reply – You can manage by filling the time with what other women refer to as housework....... darling x

SJ – Housework? Sorry the word is not familiar to me....... darling! x

B – SJ, you are right and Ian is right. I'm missing the blog already, but I know what he means about housework, SM has the same problem!

SJ – Well done Ian, nearly there – fantastic achievement. Enjoy the train journey home, you can have a proper rest at last xxx

I'm sitting in Wetherspoons enjoying lunch...16 or 18 miles left, depending on who you ask, and looking over the forthcoming football seasons fixtures thanks to B, AL and MP. I'm envisaging getting to John O'Groats for about 4 pm.

Surely even I can do it from here!

So here I am – sitting at the John O'Groats visitor centre. I've had the obligatory photo by the sign post and the very kind gentleman took £18 off me for his trouble. Mind you it's express service, you can expect to receive the photo in around two to three weeks!

But that's it...I've covered the best part of 900 miles and I've cycled from the very south west tip of England to the very north east tip of Scotland and whoever designed the last two miles to be downhill is a bloody genius (I think it may have been God, or Jesus or Moses…I'm not even sure if they weren't all the same person!)

It's quite interesting here because it's busy and there are three lots of people…there's the American tourists who are just being their normal selves walking about slapping everyone on the back and talking to anyone who'll listen…then there's the cyclists about to set off on their JOGLE trip…they seem to be buzzing and full of adrenalin, again wanting to talk to anybody who'll listen and then there's those who have just finished LEJOG…some whom I feel I know because we've passed each other at various points on route, some whom I've seen for the first time now I'm here…and without exception, this group is quiet…you have a polite handshake, a well done and then people just walk away to be on their own, get a cup of tea, a beer, etc… I wouldn't call it subdued but it's more of a "I know you know how hard this is and you've done it. You don't need me telling you about it so just enjoy the fact that you've finished".

I'd like to just give a quick mention to the bike at this stage because it has gotten me here without any dramas. One or two people that I've met on the way had afternoons free because they were having their bikes serviced halfway…well that seemed daft to me, why wouldn't a bike last 12 days without needing looking at… I've had a bike in the past for 10 years without it ever needing "a service"…but, like I knew that I didn't need a map, it seems that experience counts for a lot and by the time I got here, the bike was making various clicks, squeaks and creaks and the back brake cable was stretched to the point of almost not working. But it got me here. No punctures and no broken spokes (which is apparently a common problem, so common that some end to enders take spare ones with them…for me, I can't fathom out how on earth you'd break a spoke just riding a bike normally).

I'd like to finish by thanking everyone who has read the blogs and those who have donated to the charities I have been raising money for and also thank you to those who have commented and sent me various messages of support over the last 12 days. And if you read the book and enjoyed it, please don't pass it on to anyone else. A proportion of the cost of each book will be going to the charities mentioned at the start of the book, so rather than pass this version on, please buy them a copy….imagine the difference we could make if everyone who had read this book bought two of their friends a copy? Or send them a link to the ebook version

So what next? Well, I've got three trains home tomorrow to negotiate first but all this lubing up every day has had me thinking…cycling's never been my pastime…swimming has been the main thing I do to keep fit (no jibes about not going very often, thank you) and that David Walliams bloke got to lube up his whole body when he swam the channel…I mean how hard can it be?

All done

AL – *Well done bloke. Just about to leave work and was wondering if you'd made it yet. Fantastic achievement, especially without any support team taking your stuff ahead for you. The bloke who I work with had a 3-man support team helping him and gave himself a hernia, although he did finish 5 days faster than you!*

Get ya sen a beer bloke, you deserve it.

LJ – *Well done, hope you have a good journey home. So!... Swimming the channel is the next challenge then?*

JA – *Well done Ian – a fantastic achievement. Just let*

me know when you are collecting sponsorship for the channel swim…

PM – *Fantastic achievement Ian. Congratulations.*

EW – *Great achievement Ian. The photos tell a story – ignorant smiling at Lands End and a more "seen it all" look at John O'Groats.*
Well done to you and the bike.

CH – *Fantastic achievement. Very well done sir. I'll admit it, I had my doubts that you'd make it after your declared lack of training. It just seemed like too big an ask. In fact, I thought there was more chance of that bloke who sits next to us singing songs about James O'Connor.*
Swimming the Channel? Geeor.

SJ – *Bet you're wishing now that you'd gone for the blonde bimbo, tattoo and motor bike option!!! Well done what a fantastic achievement. Can't wait to see the photos (honest) make sure you get plenty of rest on the train & we'll see you tomorrow. Ben's got the wickets up ready!*

My reply – *Stumps SJ, Stumps…how many times do we have to tell you they are called stumps not wickets!*

MP – *Well Done Ian, to say that we are impressed would be a massive understatement. Have a relaxing train journey home tomorrow. Well Done & Best Regards L & M*
PS Your lawn needs cutting!

Appendix – Blog Posters

Work friends and colleagues

JK – Work colleague via the Nottingham office

PB – Work colleague via the Manchester office, golf buddy and work event drinking mate

LJ – Work colleague via the Milton Keynes office

GW – Managing Director at work based mainly in Milton Keynes

DL – My immediate boss at work based mainly in Manchester.

BB – Managing Director of one of the main partners at work based in Maidenhead

EW – Work colleague via the Nottingham office

RM – Work colleague via the Milton Keynes office

Friends since school

AL – Friends since we were at primary school and watch Wednesday home and away together with our sons

CH – Friends since we were at primary school and have season tickets at Hillsborough next to each other together with our sons

B – Friends since the 6th form at school. Bought and renovated a house together for three years in our early 20s

SM – Friends since the 6th form at school. Married to B

More recent social circle

PW – Friends and golf buddies for 30 years. Met through my wife

AW – Friends for 20 years. Married to PW

PM – Friends and golf buddies for 30 years. Met through my wife

AM – Friends for 30 years. Met through my wife. Married to PM

DS – Friends and golf buddies for 30 years. Met through my wife

ST – Friends for 30 years. Met through my wife.

ABX – Friends for 30 years. Met through my wife.

JA – Friends for 30 years. Met through my wife.

STw – Work colleague of most of the above and met on various social outings and would now consider a friend.

Friends through the kid's football team that I managed

JS – Mum of one of the kids in the under 13 football team

AB – Mum of one of the kids in the under 13 football team

CP – Primary school teacher of many of the kids who always came to watch them and became a good friend

MC – Committee member at the football club

SP – Founder and committee member of the football club

Others

SJ – My wife

MP – My next-door neighbour

JL – Son of AL

Lightning Source UK Ltd.
Milton Keynes UK
UKHW050302301222
414560UK00010B/129

9 781398 471382